Managing Executive Transitions

A Guide for Nonprofits

TIM WOLFRED

Praise for *Managing Executive Transitions*

"This book offers multiple perspectives and tools for guiding an organization through an executive leadership transition. For the price of a single book, readers will find all the information normally offered in a $1,000 three-day training."

—*Suzanne Maas, Partner, Leadership Transitions*

"It's all here: A step-by-step model with easy to use guidelines and tools that cover every piece of the transition process. This resource will help boards of directors sleep better at night."

—*Nancy Fuhrman, Vice-President of Consulting,*
Executive Service Corps of Chicago

"*Managing Executive Transitions* can save nonprofit organizations thousands of hours of frustration, work, and funding. Tim Wolfred demystifies and depersonalizes the leadership transition process by offering doable strategies, factual information, and practical examples."

—*Marta T. Rosa, President, MTR Management Consulting Services*

"This book should be required reading for every executive director and board chair whether they are anticipating a transition or not. Tim Wolfred provides perspectives and insights that will help organizations be more sustainable."

—*Bryan Orander, President, Charitable Advisors, LLC*

"This is a remarkably comprehensive book. Examples, templates, and sample documents give organizations all the how-to tools needed to move forward with a transition. While no two leadership successions are alike, readers will find guidance here for organizations of all sizes."

—*Alene Valkanas, Principal, Evergreen Transitions, and*
Executive Director Emeritus, Illinois Arts Alliance

"Finally, a comprehensive compendium that brings together the wisdom and experience of Tim Wolfred and CompassPoint. This guide can help organizations normalize a 'not normal' time."

—*Nancy Jackson, Consultant, Gammy Bird Consulting*

"Even though a leadership transition is stressful and time-consuming for an organization, this book helps readers recognize that new leadership also provides a unique opportunity for change and growth."

—*Jay Zlotnick, former Executive Director, Buckelew Programs*

Managing Executive Transitions

A Guide for Nonprofits

TIM WOLFRED

Senior Projects Director
CompassPoint Nonprofit Services

FIELDSTONE
ALLIANCE

SAINT PAUL
MINNESOTA

Copyright 2009 CompassPoint Nonprofit Services

Managing Executive Transitions: A Guide for Nonprofits is one of a series of works published by Fieldstone Alliance in partnership with CompassPoint Nonprofit Services. Together, we hope to strengthen the impact of nonprofit organizations and the people who work and volunteer for them as they strive to make our communities more vital and our democracy more just.

Other titles in this series include:
The Accidental Techie by Sue Bennett et al.
Best of the Board Café by Jan Masaoka
Financial Leadership for Nonprofits Executives
    by Jeanne Bell and Elizabeth Schaffer

Fieldstone Alliance is committed to strengthening the performance of the nonprofit sector. Through the syn-ergy of its consulting, training, publishing, and research and demonstration projects, Fieldstone Alliance provides solutions to issues facing nonprofits, funders, and the communities they serve. Fieldstone Alliance was formerly Wilder Publishing and Wilder Consulting departments of the Amherst H. Wilder Foundation. For information about other Fieldstone Alliance publications, see the last page of this book. If you would like more information about Fieldstone Alliance and our services, please contact Fieldstone Alliance at

www.FieldstoneAlliance.org

Edited by Vincent Hyman Editorial Services
Designed by Ann Sudmeier, BookMobile Design and
    Publishing Services, Minneapolis, Minnesota
Manufactured in the USA
First printing, May 2009

Library of Congress Cataloging-in-Publication Data

Wolfred, Tim, 1945–
    Managing executive transitions : a guide for nonprofits / by Tim Wolfred. — 1st ed.
        p.   cm.
    Includes bibliographical references and index.
    ISBN 978-0-940069-57-2 (pbk.)
    1. Nonprofit organizations—Management.
2. Chief executive officers.   I. Title.
    HD62.6.W653 2009
    658.4'07—dc22

                            2008055092

ISBN 978-1-68442-203-6 (hc)

Contents

List of Tools   vii
About the Author   ix
About CompassPoint Nonprofit Services   ix
Acknowledgments   xi

Introduction   1
Goals of the Book   2
Who This Book Is For   3
How to Use This Book   4
Where to Start Reading   6

Chapter One: *Leadership Transitions as Opportunities for Agency Renewal*   **9**
Model and Rationale   9
Types of Transitions   14

Chapter Two: *Essential Elements of a Successful Leadership Transition*   **23**
The Three Phases of Executive Transition Management   23
The Essential Elements for a Successful Transition   26

Chapter Three: *Prepare*   **31**
Getting Organized   31
Updating the Agency's Leadership Agenda   44
Creating the Candidate Profile   58

Chapter Four: *Pivot*   **61**
Upgrading Organizational Capacity   61
Attending to Staff Transition Needs   62
The Search   63
Screening and Hiring   77

Chapter Five: *Thrive*   **103**
Getting Started   103
Orientation   104
Performance Goals and Evaluation   107
Building the Board and Executive Team   114
Professional Development for the New Executive   116

Chapter Six: *Transition Topics* **119**

    Considerations for the Long-Tenured Executive   119
    The Role of the Departing Executive   123
    Dealing with Internal Candidates   125
    Crafting Exit Packages   126
    Grooming a Successor   127
    Embracing Diversity and Difference   128
    Using an Interim Executive Director   129
    Choosing and Using Consultants and Recruiters   131

Afterword   **135**

Appendix A: *Stepping Up: A Board's Challenge in Leadership Transition*   **139**

Appendix B: *Emergency Succession-Planning Template*   **149**

    Emergency Succession Plan   149

Appendix C: *Resources*   **155**

    Web Sites   155
    Bibliography   156

Notes   **159**

Index   **161**

Tools

Tool 1: *Sample Agenda for First Meeting of the Transition Committee*   37
Tool 2: *Sample Timeline & Work Plan*   40
Tool 3: *Communications Plan: First Letter to Stakeholders*   45
Tool 4: *Board Survey Questions*   47
Tool 5: *Board Self-Assessment Survey*   48
Tool 6: *Sample Staff Survey*   50
Tool 7: *Sample Questions for Community Interviews*   52
Tool 8: *Creating the Leadership Agenda and Candidate Profile*   55
Tool 9: *Sample Leadership Agenda*   56
Tool 10: *Candidate Profile*   60
Tool 11: *Attending to Staff's Transition through All Three Phases*   64
Tool 12: *Sample Job Announcement*   67
Tool 13: *Sample Recruitment Plan*   68
Tool 14: *Sample Memo to Board and Staff on Networking*   74
Tool 15: *Summary of Typical Screening Sequence*   78
Tool 16: *Sample Letter of Acknowledgment to Applicants*   79
Tool 17: *Examples of First-Round Interview Questions*   82
Tool 18: *Behavioral Interviewing*   85
Tool 19: *Sample Candidate Rating Form*   88
Tool 20: *Checking References*   91
Tool 21: *Sample Agenda for Finalists' Interviews and Decision-Making Meeting*   95
Tool 22: *Making a Choice*   97
Tool 23: *Offer Letter Template*   99
Tool 24: *Rejection Letter to Applicants Not Interviewed*   100
Tool 25: *Hiring Announcement Letter*   105
Tool 26: *Sample New Executive Director Orientation Plan*   106
Tool 27: *Sample Set of Executive Performance Goals*   108
Tool 28: *Executive Director Annual Assessment Form*   110

About the Author

Before founding the Executive Transitions program at CompassPoint Nonprofit Services in 1997, Tim Wolfred served sixteen times as interim executive director of San Francisco Bay Area nonprofits. Tim began his nonprofit career in 1971 as executive director of an Illinois child welfare agency. He was an early organizer of local and national responses to the AIDS epidemic as executive director of the San Francisco AIDS Foundation from 1985 to 1989. He is coauthor of two seminal studies of nonprofit executive director tenure and experience, *Daring to Lead* (2001 with Jeanne Peters) and *Daring to Lead 2006* (with Jeanne Bell and Richard Moyers). Both studies were published by CompassPoint. He has also written two monographs in a series on executive transition issues published by the Annie E. Casey Foundation, *Interim Executive Directors: The Power in the Middle* and *Building Leaderful Organizations: Succession Planning for Nonprofits*. With training partner Karen Gaskins Jones of JLH Associates, Tim created a three-day workshop for nonprofit consultants on the use of the transition model presented in this book. More than 150 consultants across the country have been through the training over the past four years.

About CompassPoint Nonprofit Services

CompassPoint Nonprofit Services is a nonprofit consulting, education, and research organization with offices in San Francisco and Silicon Valley, California. Through a broad range of services and initiatives, CompassPoint serves nonprofit volunteers and staff with the tools, concepts, and strategies necessary to shape change in leadership, nonprofit strategy, finance, fundraising, governance, and executive transition management. CompassPoint frequently publishes books, articles, and research reports on topics of relevance to nonprofits, funders, and capacity builders. For more information, visit www.compasspoint.org.

Acknowledgments

The author wishes to acknowledge several valued colleagues who have contributed to the body of knowledge and practice that is detailed in this book:

▷ The members of CompassPoint's executive transitions consulting group, past and present, who with the author molded many of the tools and protocols in this book: Mim Carlson, Viveka Chen, Margaret Donohoe, Natasha D'Silva, Kerry Enright, Anushka Fernandopulle, Byron Johnson, Diane Johnson, Ken Kurtzig, Karen Robbins, Amari Romero-Thomas, Ted Scott, Debbie Wu, and J. R. Yeager.

▷ Visionary leaders Jan Masaoka and Mike Allison, who first conceived of an executive transitions service during their tenure at CompassPoint and brought the resources and people together to create it.

▷ The consultants of TransitionGuides, especially Tom Adams and Don Tebbe, who were critically important thought partners with the author as the Executive Transitions Management model was being codified. Tom gets a special founder's recognition for having created an early prototype for the ETM model in his work for the Neighborhood Reinvestment Corporation (now NeighborWorks America) in the 1990s.

The author especially thanks the Evelyn and Walter Haas, Jr. Fund for generously underwriting a large portion of his time in writing this book, for being readily available over the years for advice and counsel as the executive transitions program at CompassPoint has evolved, and for promoting to the nonprofit sector the benefits of a thoughtful approach to leadership turnovers.

The author also appreciates enormously the early and ongoing leadership and financial support of the Annie E. Casey Foundation. The Casey Foundation has generously funded CompassPoint and others, both for the creation of this practical model for assisting nonprofits with their transitions and for promoting its availability. The foundation has underwritten the training of more than 150 transition consultants from all parts of the country and has funded transition assistance for its grantees.

And, very importantly, the author owes a huge debt of gratitude to Cristina Chan, the publications director at CompassPoint Nonprofit Services. Cristina did her best to keep him on task and on time and provided invaluable editorial assistance throughout the writing process.

Introduction

This book presents the executive transition practices and tools as they've been honed by CompassPoint consultants over the past decade with more than three hundred nonprofit organizations.

CompassPoint Nonprofit Services created its Executive Transitions program in 1997 in response to seeing so many nonprofit agencies struggle with their leadership turnovers. Community agencies, especially medium-sized and smaller ones, were having trouble getting the help they needed to recruit good candidates to succeed their departing executives. The available search services were often unaffordable. And while most local corporate recruiters did great work in the for-profit sector, they weren't often attuned to the culture of community-based nonprofits, where broad staff inclusion in decision making and a nonmonetary bottom line were highly valued. The majority of nonprofit boards were left to their own devices, often relying on a board member or two who had some sort of recruiting experience in their day jobs.

I was recruited to CompassPoint after having served as an interim executive for some sixteen organizations. I now lead a group of eight transition consultants. The CompassPoint team has assembled a transition toolkit containing over two hundred items, some of which are featured in this book. The transition framing, tools, and advice in this book have been created and honed through my interim executive experience and in our client work at CompassPoint.

Our CompassPoint practice was inspired initially by the pioneering work of Tom Adams in the 1990s at what is now NeighborWorks America. And, importantly, our practice has been augmented over the years through learning exchanges with TransitionGuides, Tom's current Maryland-based firm. The work of Third Sector New England in Boston has been a further influence.

I've further developed ideas about transition leadership by teaching other consultants. With funding support from the Annie E. Casey Foundation, Karen Gaskins Jones of JLH Associates and I created a three-day training for nonprofit consultants interested in our transition specialty. More than 150 transition consultants from across the country have enthusiastically received the training; the wisdom they've derived from their own client work has served to further inform this book.

CompassPoint's practices have also been influenced by the experiences of nonprofit executive transition programs that started up across the country in more recent years. An affinity group of nonprofit transition practitioners, some fifty strong, now meets annually as an adjunct to the annual conference of the Alliance for Nonprofit Management and gathers by phone on a regular basis to share client learnings.

In addition to these resources, CompassPoint has explored the existing authors on leadership transitions, such as Tom Gilmore,[1] and sought the counsel of William Bridges, a leading thinker and author on the topic of change management.[2]

The need for this book is heightened by recent data on the projected rate of nonprofit executive turnovers. CompassPoint's national survey of about two thousand executive directors found 75 percent of them stating they planned to leave their jobs in five years or less.[3] Similar surveys report between 45 percent and 75 percent expecting to resign within five years.[4] In addition, we expect to soon see the departure of baby boomers who came into the nonprofit sector in big numbers in the 1960s and 1970s, many as the founding executives of their agencies.

If these projections are accurate, a majority of nonprofit boards will be faced with executive transitions in their agencies in the near future. This book is a guide for managing these leadership turnovers. And even if a board has the resources to hire outside transition help at the moment of transition, this book will help it gain an advance perspective on how to manage leadership turnovers in ways that can heighten mission impact while avoiding potential downsides.

Goals of the Book

This book provides a framework and tools that nonprofit agencies can use to manage their executive leadership transitions and to seize the opportunities inherent in such transitions.

A leadership transition at the top can be a time of high vulnerability for an agency. Will donors leave with the executive who cultivated them? Will foundations that have invested in the agency's programs pull back? Will programs stay on track and on budget? Will finances suffer?

On the other hand, the moment of executive turnover offers unique opportunities for renewal and fresh thinking. As one search consultant phrased it: "When the executive director leaves, things become a bit unglued." This unglued state offers board and staff members a chance to put things back together in new and creative ways—to discard some old pieces and to bring in fresh elements. Our clients have used this transition period to create new visions, to solve old problems, and to energize supporters, in addition to searching for and selecting promising new leaders.

We believe that a robust nonprofit sector is critical to a vibrant national democracy. Community-led and community-based agencies established to address acknowledged civic needs are important vehicles for community health, expression, and creativity. Nonprofit agencies at their best are groups of citizens energized by a shared vision of a healthy community and invested in making it real.

We hope this book will equip nonprofit organizations with the skills and knowledge to manage the vulnerabilities that can emerge from an executive departure. We hope nonprofits will take full advantage of the tremendous opportunities transition presents—opportunities to take a fresh look at community needs, to update program strategies, and to build new excitement for their work.

Who This Book Is For

The primary audience for this book is the boards of directors of community nonprofit agencies. More than one million groups in this country are incorporated as "community benefit" organizations—501(c)(3)s, 501(c)(4)s, and others. The board most likely to use this book oversees an agency with a budget of up to $10 million; this includes the vast majority of nonprofits in the United States.

One of the chief duties of a board is to hire, monitor, and support its agency's chief executive. Many boards, at the point of turnover, set out with the routine approach used for hiring any employee: advertise the position, screen resumes, interview candidates, check references, make a choice, and negotiate the terms of employment.

But the majority hit significant bumps and potholes along the way:[5] The departing executive has a candidate she is aggressively promoting in the face of board skepticism. Staff doesn't trust the board to hire the right person and morale dips. A funder decides to withhold a renewal grant pending a chance to vet the next executive, creating a financial crisis. The board gets into a prolonged debate over which of two finalists to hire.

While, first and foremost, this book is for boards of directors, other audiences will find it helpful. Executive directors looking for advice on how to prepare their organizations for their departures and for information on their appropriate roles in the process will make good use of the steps and protocols presented. At the point of announcing their departures to their boards, they may want to offer this book as a practical transition guide. Similarly, managers in community agencies can learn best practices and see how to best channel their input into the work of renewing their agency's visions and strategies and in choosing new leaders.

Funders can offer this book as a guide to grantees that are about to enter an executive transition and as a template against which to evaluate the transition grant requests they receive from community groups. We believe that funders must not pull back and compound the problems that agencies face when their leaders depart. Rather, by offering transition support that results in an agency's renewal, funders can enhance the program investments they've already made in that agency.

How to Use This Book

The sections of this book lead readers through the entire journey of Executive Transition Management (ETM). The book starts by framing the rationale of executive transitions and then provides an overview of the model, followed by an in-depth explanation of each step of the transition process. Various organizational context issues that impact the ETM process are factored in.

Chapter One, "Leadership Transitions as Opportunities for Agency Renewal," presents the rationale and change management theory that underpin the executive transitions model and its related tools. The rationale includes the values and principles that inform the model—in other words, the whys behind the hows.

The chapter follows with a listing of the various types of executive transitions experienced by nonprofit agencies at different points in their life cycle—from a *start-up,* in which a board is hiring its first executive director, to the *high-performing agency* whose primary concern is not losing momentum when its leader departs, to a *turnaround* transition that requires significant attention to repairing systems and relationships that have gone awry, to agencies facing special complexities of separating from founders and long-term leaders—the *heroes and heroines* of the nonprofit sector.

For each type of transition, a brief case example from CompassPoint's experiences is presented. A listing of the unique factors typically present in each of these transitions that need careful attention and emphasis is included.

Chapter Two, "Essential Elements of a Successful Leadership Transition," opens with an overview of the three major phases in our executive transitions model. The phases take an agency from the moment its executive announces her intention to resign through the first few months of the next executive's tenure. It starts with how to make for a "good ending" with the departing leader and moves through all the work necessary to make for a "good beginning" with the successor. The high-level goal for the work is a successful tenure for the new leader that advances the agency's mission and community impact. Chapter Two concludes with a listing of what CompassPoint considers to be the essential elements of a healthy leadership transition.

This overview is followed by three chapters that describe in greater depth and detail the specific activities to be undertaken in each phase of transition. Chapter Three, "Prepare," covers the series of recommended steps a board can take to prepare for a successful leadership transition, such as updating the agency's vision and strategic directions. Chapter Four, "Pivot," addresses the search and selection process, as well as some of the internal organizational capacity-building that agencies can pay attention to during their transition. Chapter Five, "Thrive," discusses processes agencies can use to ease a new executive into his job and the organization. It also covers ways to set a strong foundation for moving forward, such as setting appropriate performance goals for the newly hired executive.

These prescribed steps are accompanied by tools agencies can use in their transition work. Developed by CompassPoint's consultants, the tools can be modified to fit specific needs. Among the tools and resources presented are guidelines for how the transition and search committee should be constituted, as well as a generic job description for the committee chair. There are sample questions for interviewing "key informants" in pursuit of information on an agency's strengths, challenges, and future directions. There are questions for screening executive candidates. And finally there are tools for use in launching the newly hired executive in ways that set him up for success as the new leader of an organization.

Chapter Six, "Transition Topics," catalogs some of the common topics related to transition encountered with clients. Not every topic will be relevant to every agency's particular transition, but it still may be useful to skim them. Agencies might catch an issue that it needs to consider, but hasn't. For agencies facing a gap between executives, there's a discussion of interim executive directors—the skills needed, what to expect of them, and how to screen them. "Considerations for the Long-Tenured Executive" will be of value to boards whose founding executives (or long-term executives) are leaving. If the board is looking to hire a consultant or recruiting firm, there's advice on how to pick one that's a good fit for the organization.

Additional help is available in the appendices. Appendix A is a reprint of an article on the board's challenge during leadership transition. Appendix B is a template for an emergency succession plan, which an organization can study and modify in preparation for the sudden loss, temporary or permanent, of its executive. Finally, Appendix C provides a list of useful web and print resources.

Where to Start Reading

This guide is meant to be modular. Do a quick scan to figure out where your organization is and go to the section most pertinent to your immediate needs. Following are the sections most immediately useful for boards, executive directors, interim executive directors, and consultants.

For Board Members

Board members need to understand the book's transition concepts and advice (Chapters One and Two) to be able to address the board's duty to manage risk. Your executive may have no foreseeable plans to leave, but an unforeseen event could cause a sudden departure. It might be a health crisis, poaching by an executive headhunter, or a winning lottery ticket. Foreknowledge of the tricky dynamics of an executive transition can prevent hasty actions and mistakes that aggravate an emergency situation rather than contain the possible damage that can ensue from the leadership crisis.

If your executive has just announced that she is leaving in three months, you can use the first two chapters to organize your thoughts as you begin to design your board's process for seeking a successor. As you execute your plan, refer to the tools in Chapters Three, Four, and Five for advice on addressing a particular facet of your transition. In Chapter Six there are tips on what to look for in an interim executive director and where to find candidates for your temporary executive position.

Chapter Four could be the place to start if you're picking up this book in the middle of an executive transition. You've just finished recruiting a pool of executive candidates, for example, and you need some advice and tools on how to screen their resumes and set up interviews. Or if you've just hired your new executive director and want a sample plan for starting her off on the right foot, you would go to Chapter Five.

In a related vein, executive succession planning has come to the forefront as an important element in an agency's strategic plan. It speaks to the wave of baby boomers who founded agencies twenty-five years ago and to an era of shorter tenures (three to seven years on average) for a newer generation of nonprofit leaders. The central strategic focus is on goals for building bench strength by making sure that an executive's key leadership and management duties are backed up by other staff. The section "Considerations for the Long-Tenured Executive" on page 119 in Chapter Six describes three types of succession planning you might undertake. Your strategic plan might additionally speak to framing the protocol the board would follow, maybe years down the road, at the point the executive sets a departure date. Chapter Two of this book, "Essential Elements of a Successful Leadership Transition," can be a reference for designing that protocol.

For Executive Directors

If you're an executive director contemplating a change in jobs, you might start in Chapter Six with the section "Role of the Departing Executive." At the point of telling your board chair that you have decided to resign, you might excerpt the "Model and Rationale" section in Chapter One, which highlights the opportunities available to a board in a transition, and all of Chapter Two ("Essential Elements of a Successful Leadership Transition") to help the chair begin thinking about how to lead the leadership turnover process. Or, if you're an executive who's on the job until your successor is ready to start, you could have the tools in Chapter Three available as needed by your board.

For Interim Executive Directors

As an interim executive director, you could find this guide a helpful resource as you support a board in its work to identify the next permanent agency leader. Interim leadership is a burgeoning specialty in the nonprofit sector. The temporary leader who approaches the job as a capacity-building opportunity for the client agency (Chapter One) has the greatest chance of setting up the organization for an exciting and productive future.

For Consultants

Consultants often encounter a client moving into a leadership change. Understanding the renewal opportunities in the change (Chapter One) will help you advise the client on positive framing that can mitigate anxieties. Knowing best practices for moving through a transition (Chapter Two) will allow you to advise the client on making good choices regarding contracting for transition assistance.

For All Readers

For all users of this guide, the tools and advice in Chapters Two, Three, and Four can provide the opportunity to go deeper into a particular transition activity, such as clarifying an agency's strategic directions (Chapter Three), candidate recruitment techniques (Chapter Four), or how to support a new executive in the first few months of his tenure (Chapter Five).

Whatever your role with a community nonprofit that's undergoing or preparing to undergo an executive turnover, you will find advice and tools in this guide that will help that agency prevent the difficulties and maximize the opportunities inherent in what is a major event in any agency's life.

Chapter One:

Leadership Transitions as Opportunities for Agency Renewal

▷ This first chapter offers an overview of the context and rationale for executive transition followed by a brief outline of the steps an organization can expect to engage in as a part of this process. We address the four main types of nonprofit executive transition that we have encountered. These types are largely determined by where an organization is in its life cycle. Four case studies illustrate these various transition types.

Model and Rationale

A nonprofit leadership transition, diligently undertaken, provides a rich opportunity for agency renewal and for reenergizing all parties central to the agency's success. It's one door to assuring that your agency has the greatest impact.

Most people join the nonprofit sector out of a passion for doing something about a community need—taking on an injustice, enriching the cultural environment, improving the natural environment, or mending a hole in the social fabric. People give of their talents and time because they want to have a positive impact on the world around them.

The protocols for managing nonprofit executive transitions presented in this guide have been designed with the central goal of promoting greater mission impact. The Executive Transition Management model, as we call it—or ETM for short—promotes *transformational* activities for nonprofits at the point their current leader is leaving. We believe a more static approach is merely *transactional*. One leader departs the executive chair and the board goes through a set of steps to put a new leader in that chair. The ETM process encourages a look at the transformational changes an agency might make to enhance program outcomes.

The transformational activities of the ETM process are organized into three phases: *Prepare, Pivot,* and *Thrive.* The Prepare phase engages board members, staff, volunteers, and funders in an efficient process for updating the agency's strategic directions. The fresh directions are based on a review of current community needs. The agency then checks its systems for its capacity to successfully pursue those directions. It sets goals for system upgrades where needed. And then, based on these directions and the identified capacity-building needs, the agency crafts a profile of the skills and attributes needed in the next executive. Staff participate in setting the direction and give input to the candidate profile. They will have also acknowledged the achievements of the preceding executive and gained closure with her tenure. They're now excited about moving forward with a new staff leader. In the Pivot phase, a search ensues, conducted by a board reinvigorated and excited about the agency's future impact. Simultaneous with the search, the agency takes on some of the needed capacity upgrades highlighted in the earlier systems check—for example, bringing financial management systems up to par with existing industry standards. In the Thrive phase the board engages the newly hired executive as a leadership partner and gives her clear performance priorities derived from the strategic directions.

William Bridges has written extensively on the topic of change management over a thirty-year career of consulting to corporate leaders. His book *Managing Transitions: Making the Most of Change* provides prescriptions for successfully leading change and mining it for growth opportunities; some elements of the ETM model are built on his work.[6]

Bridges conceptualizes change proceeding through three successive phases. The process starts the moment an upcoming change is first conceived. This is the *ending* phase, a period of letting go of the old. It then moves into a *neutral zone,* during which work is done to bring the new into focus, while attachments to the old fade. The neutral zone is a time of anxiety and maybe chaos as the known ground of the old has been left and the new ground is not yet underfoot. But it's the unsettledness and the chaos that present the opportunity for creativity, for designing the new ground differently. It's a time to decide what elements of the old should be carried forward and what new elements to incorporate. Bridges notes that to rush through the neutral zone to escape the discomfort is also to miss the opportunity for creativity. The final phase is the *beginning,* the arrival of the new ground. It's a time of excitement and fresh energy as staff enter and embrace the new era.

Several axioms for moving successfully through a change emerge from this model.

The first axiom is *you can't have a beginning without an ending.* To the degree that you're holding on to the old, you'll have trouble embracing the new. The quality of the new beginning is dependent to a large measure on the quality and completeness of the ending.

The second axiom is *don't rush through the neutral zone if you want to make the most of the change opportunities.* On the other hand, you don't want to hang out there too long. While folks are in the neutral zone, they're going to be off-kilter and anxious; strange behaviors may emerge and should be considered a natural occurrence in the neutral zone. Leaders need to be aware of and make allowances for the natural turbulence in the change process. They also need to keep the group moving toward the new ground by facilitating processes for letting go of the old and for envisioning the inviting shape of the new.

The final axiom is *individuals in a group will move through the three transition phases at widely varying speeds.* Some will drop the old quickly and immediately grasp the exciting opportunities in the new. Others will continue to grieve the loss of the old long after most have firmly engaged the new.

In applying the Bridges framework to an executive transition, the ETM model is careful to make for good endings with the departing executive director. He is fully acknowledged for the achievements of his tenure and for sacrifices made in pursuit of the agency mission. Good-bye rituals help board and staff to let go of the executive and the executive to gain closure on his tenure. The executive physically separates from the agency facility and serves in any ongoing role with the agency completely at the behest of the next executive. Space is made for a good beginning with the new leader.

Before starting an executive search, a board is urged to hang out in the neutral zone a bit to take stock of current operations and to look at how the agency might have greater impact in the community it serves. This impact review generates a picture of the kind of executive the agency needs going forward.

Acknowledging the critical advantages to taking stock between leaders, some Protestant denominations mandate that their congregations take time out for reflection on the departure of a permanent pastor. The denominations maintain a corps of interim pastors specially trained to facilitate that creative process. The interim's work includes helping the church members to set goals for the future and to identify the skills the next pastor will need to lead them toward those goals. The interim period also gives the congregation time to psychologically detach from the previous pastor, experience a different leadership style with the interim, and get excited about a new future under new guidance.

After the hire is made, the ETM model focuses on the new beginning. The new executive and board set the parameters for how they'll work together as the leadership team for the agency. They come to agreement on the initial performance objectives for the executive and what support and resources he may need in pursuing them. Similarly, the executive engages with the management team in making explicit how they will lead the agency together and meld their individual leadership styles. The executive shares his performance objectives with the team and negotiates the tasks of each manager in helping to reach the goals.

Another key feature of Bridges's model is his view that any change event has both a *change* element and a *transition* element. Changes are relatively concrete events of short duration, such as the move to a new city, the installation of a new software system, the death of a loved one. In contrast, transitions are the psychological and emotional accompaniments to any change. Transitions are less tangible and can be of much longer duration, such as getting comfortable living in a new city, getting beyond the anxiety and frustration involved in using new software, or grieving the loss of a loved one.

Bridges states that failure to attend to the transition side of any change and failure to acknowledge that feelings and frustrations have any validity can derail the change. Denied or pushed down, anger and grief can be prolonged. Conscious or unconscious sabotage of the change can result. Depression may set in.

In a nonprofit leadership change, there will be feelings on all sides related to the departure of the executive. Staff may need to grieve the departure of a beloved leader or move through resentments that had built up with an underperforming executive who was asked to leave. The ETM process includes ways for staff to celebrate and to gain closure with the beloved leader. This includes truly listening to and acknowledging staff grievances, hopes, and expectations.

The need to be proactive in helping staff move through their transitions is a major reason that the ETM model urges that staff be actively involved with the board in the neutral zone activities rather than be outsiders to a board process. For instance, we recommend that staff representatives be on the board's transition and search committee and that those representatives bring staff input to the committee. We suggest limits to staff roles, but a relatively deep involvement by staff facilitates their letting go of the old and embracing new directions and new leadership. The next executive will have a staff better prepared to move forward with him.

And the departing executive will have a mixture of feelings: great joy in what has been accomplished, relief in letting go of a burdensome administrative load, guilt over leaving the cause, sadness in separating from staff, or anxiety in not knowing what's next. Again, the transition leaders need to acknowledge there are emotions involved in the change and the executive needs a chance to move through them.

A leadership change is a big event in the life of a nonprofit and one that touches all parties. Change is tough; the transition leader realizes it's a time of heightened emotions. Everyone—board, staff, departing executive—will be to some degree anxious and on edge. Some "acting out" is expected, as individuals sometimes deal with stress in dysfunctional ways. Heightened emotionality is natural. Through a conscious and deliberate transition process, foreseeable acting out will be less likely to disrupt the transition.

The ETM model obviously calls for deep involvement of the board. In the model the board will have given serious thought about strategic directions for the agency and will get a clear picture of current operations and capacity. The process should deepen board members' commitment to the agency, bring them closer to staff, and build their enthusiasm for the future.

The specific steps included in the ETM model for moving through a leadership change are detailed in Chapter Two. Employing Bridges's concepts, the steps include activities for ensuring a good ending with the ways and personality of the departing executive, for taking advantage of the neutral zone, and for having a good beginning with fresh strategic directions and a new leader. Attention is given to the transition side of the leadership change as well, specifically to personal needs that are critical to a successful start with new leadership.

The ETM process presented in this guide is a somewhat complex and idealized recipe for making a successful leadership transition. No agency has ever followed it completely and exactly. All agencies modify it to fit their needs, their particular agency cultures, and their resources. The author hopes, however, that this guide provides sufficient advice and tools to help agencies big and small, with boards large or compact, to seize the opportunities for building agency capacity available in a leadership turnover and to avoid the catastrophic consequences of a failed transition.

Types of Transitions

The transformational needs and opportunities in an agency's move to new leadership will vary depending on where it is in its life cycle (a start-up versus a decades-old community institution) and on its current condition (humming along with solid financing versus being demoralized and having terminated the incumbent). A transition is rarely "routine," and no two have the exact same elements. But from our experience, executive transitions generally fall into one of the following categories: start-ups hiring their first staff; high-

CASE EXAMPLE:
The Treasure Island Memorial Foundation[7]

The Treasure Island Memorial Foundation had been organized ten years earlier to restore and preserve three buildings on the decommissioned naval base in San Francisco Bay as a memorial to U.S. Navy personnel who had served in World War II, the Korean War, or the Vietnam War. The all-volunteer foundation, composed primarily of Navy veterans, provided the labor to renovate the buildings and to install a museum, which offered a history of the Navy's role in the three wars.

When the foundation contacted CompassPoint, the museum had been in operation for two years and was open for visitors on weekends. Foundation board members had decided they now needed an executive director to relieve them of ever-expanding administrative functions and to execute their vision to expand the museum's size and hours of operation.

Discussion with the group revealed it had few funds to pay staff. All revenue from member donations and museum admissions went to facility costs and acquisition of museum items. With CompassPoint's counsel,

performing agencies attempting to keep up with change and growth; agencies that are in need of turnaround; and agencies that are separating from a long and strong incumbent.

The Start-up: Hiring the First Staff

The agency hiring its first executive director may just be starting operations or it may have been led by volunteers for a number of years. In either case, it needs to establish quality administrative systems that conform to regulatory statutes—in management of finances, in personnel policies, and in program delivery. In situations where the board has been the management body for a period of time, there will need to be extra attention given to the final phase of the board's transition. Letting go of administrative and program duties and delegating them to their new executives, as they become a policy body that monitors outcomes, is a difficult shift for most such boards.

the board decided its first staff hire should be a fundraiser; it could seed the position with a grant from a local foundation. To get the foundation started, CompassPoint helped it contract with a fundraising professional who filled the position on an interim basis for a year. Besides getting a fundraising plan formed and off the ground, the consultant was charged with helping the board clarify the skills needed in a permanent executive position. Additionally, the consultant acclimated the seat-of-the-pants board to what it needed to do differently to successfully hire and support professional staff.

At the end of the year, an executive director with solid fundraising credentials was hired. With a development plan and administrative systems already in place, the new staff person got off to a smooth start. With the board having already worked through most of the tensions that can arise when an all-volunteer group first delegates to paid staff, the new executive was able to quickly move forward with the board in growing the organization.

The High-Performing Agency: Keeping up with Change and Growth

The organization experiencing the change-and-growth transition has programs that are fully enrolled and regularly applauded by funders and the community. However, the high-performing agency can't rest on its laurels. It will eventually decline or find itself running to catch up to changes imposed on it by external forces. At the moment of transition, the agency needs to look around and shift goals and adopt strategies for a sustainable future that support change and keep up with demands for growth. Such shifts can involve dramatic changes in program strategies or in infrastructure.

CASE EXAMPLE:
City Center Homeless Services

Charles, a social worker, had built City Center's reputation for high-quality services to homeless families in Oakland, California, over the six years of his tenure as executive director. He had kept its finances in good order. He was moving to the East Coast to be closer to his aging parents.

The board engaged CompassPoint to provide transition and search services. The board started with the assumption that it needed another passionate social worker like Charles. But, in gathering data for the board's review of strategic directions, CompassPoint learned from interviews with City Center's funders that they were in the early stages of requiring their grantees to regionalize their homeless services. City Center's goal was to move families into family-friendly shelters and then into transitional housing, to help the adults get jobs, and finally to move them into affordable permanent housing. Increasingly that permanent housing was located two to three counties east of City Center's county, where housing costs were the highest in the region. Funders understood that service agencies needed to stick with their clients for an extended period after they relocated to permanent homes to support the families' success.

"Regionalizing" for City Center would mean either opening branch offices in neighboring counties or subcontracting with providers in those

When the shift involves changes in a successful program, the next leader will need to be adept at leading shifts in service methods, markets, geographic distribution, and populations.

When the shift involves infrastructure—for example, updating administrative systems and staff skills to catch up to the dramatic program growth fostered by the departing leader—the next executive needs to focus on expanding the capacity of financial, personnel, and technology systems that support the expanded enterprise. If not, the overstressed staff may burn out or leave. The agency is in a phase that emphasizes stabilization of recent program gains.

counties for continuation of client support. Charles had been an excellent service designer and provider within the walls of City Center, but as a social worker, he had not been trained to build collaborations with other agencies or to open distant service branches. Regionalizing, a strategic direction to be pursued by Charles's successor, would require those skill sets.

On the financial front, another new direction needed was the development of private sources of revenue. City Center was largely dependent on state and federal grants administered by the city. Not only were increased service demands straining those dollars, but the mayor was planning on diverting some of the funds to a new homeless initiative that would be city run. The next executive would have a second critical goal of acquiring funds from foundations and individual donors.

Although City Center was currently thriving under Charles's leadership, the skills profile for the next executive ended up looking quite different from Charles's due to the trends identified in the homeless services and funding environment. To maintain and build on Charles's successes, the next leader would need to be an aggressive entrepreneur, locating new revenue sources and spreading into distant communities.

Turnarounds: Reversing a Decline

In an agency in decline, things are seriously amiss. A number of difficult conditions exist. The agency is in a financial tailspin. Disappearing revenue streams have not been replaced by new sources. Expenses are out of control. Aging receivables have not been pursued. Program enrollments have dropped dramatically; services get poor reviews or are out of sync with client needs. Staff morale is low and staff turnover high. The executive has been unable to turn things around, or the executive may have been terminated.

The board's first transition task is to understand the cause of the malaise and to stabilize operations. One strategy often employed is to hire an interim executive director to organize staff and to arrange resources to steady the

CASE EXAMPLE:
New Beginnings

New Beginnings in San Jose, California, provides counseling, job training, and job hunting assistance to individuals recently released from prison. Forty percent of its $800,000 budget was covered by a grant from the U.S. Department of Labor. At the end of its three-year term, the grant was not renewed and the executive director had failed to find replacement funding. The board terminated the executive and went on crisis footing. It was forced to lay off some staff and to reduce the hours of others. The board brought in as a half-time interim executive the agency's former director of employment services, who had been very popular with his staff. The interim leader, however, had no experience with financial management and fundraising. He reluctantly accepted the temporary job out of loyalty to the agency.

CompassPoint was approached to help with an immediate search for a permanent new leader who could rescue the program. But the board, comprised entirely of former clients and grassroots activists, wasn't certain New Beginnings could pull out of its tailspin.

CompassPoint persuaded the board to put off the search and to adopt two strategies for righting the agency. The first was quickly to bring in

agency. The interim may have a several months-long contract and be charged to more completely turn around the agency. A refurbished organization will more easily draw candidates to the permanent executive position when the board later begins the recruitment. Alternatively, the board may want time with an interim executive to consider merging with another nonprofit as a way out of irresolvable financial straits.

Heroes and Heroines: Separating from a Long and Strong Incumbent

Paradoxically, executive transitions with particularly long-tenured and successful executives can be the most challenging. The stronger the ties to an executive, the greater the care needed to loosen those ties and to avoid damage to programs.

a consultant to work with the board on fundraising for big dollars. The quality of its programs and its mission had strong potential for garnering support. Lists of potential donors were drawn up and board members were trained to ask for funds. (Providentially, one of the appeals was to a local political leader who was able to get an emergency grant of $150,000 from the state employment department because of his close association with the governor.)

Second, CompassPoint recruited a seasoned nonprofit executive to serve as interim director for a nine-month contract. CompassPoint agreed it would start the search for a permanent executive six months into his term if the prospects for financial viability improved significantly by that point.

Donations and new grants were generated, and the agency returned to solid footing. And in recruiting for a permanent executive, the board was successful in bringing on a person who could lead the agency in integrating the involvement of spouses and partners of clients in activities and as support, a strategic direction established by the board when it looked to what transformations might be needed to best prepare and lay the foundation for client transition to work post-incarceration.

Typically, the highly accomplished executive (sometimes the founder) has tied her professional identity and purpose in life to leading the agency. Often the transition work begins in helping her successfully let go and ease into her next career and life phase. It also entails preparing the agency to thrive, to draw donors and funders, and to engage the commitment of staff and board beyond the strong presence of the current executive. And then it means embracing a successor who likely will lead and manage differently than the incumbent, who is often seen as a heroine by staff, board, and community for her endurance and achievements.

In the transition from a longtime, strong incumbent, a simple replacement strategy, in which the agency does nothing more than recruit and hire a successor,

CASE EXAMPLE:
Main Street Services

Dwayne had founded Main Street Services in Santa Rosa, California, twenty-seven years earlier to provide recreational and academic support programs for developmentally disabled youth living in a three-county region. The agency now had a budget of nearly $5 million and a staff of sixty working both in Main Street's large facility and in several schools throughout the region. Dwayne had decided he would leave his job in two years and begin a part-time consulting practice.

Dwayne realized that he ran the agency a bit idiosyncratically and that he was the chief rainmaker for his programs. He engaged CompassPoint to help him with his succession planning.

CompassPoint recommended several key interventions to prepare Main Street to stand strong after Dwayne's retirement. Dwayne was essentially serving as CEO, CFO, and chief fundraiser for Main Street, likely too full a plate of responsibilities for the next executive. A CFO position was created and immediately filled by an interim professional who standardized financial systems and encouraged Dwayne to let go of the minutiae of financial management. The development associate position was upgraded to director level and a search was begun to fill it.

can be fatal. With too little reflection and preparation, a successor can quickly be destroyed by the dynamics of an agency in which the long-term leader has not fully let go or in which operational weaknesses and staff deficiencies were hidden behind the towering predecessor. Anecdotes abound of agencies in which the successor's successor is the one who eventually takes hold of the nonprofit, learning from the travails that doomed the first "interim" successor.

The amount of transition work required with long-serving executives is in proportion to the dimensions of their tenure and the size of their agencies. Ideally, succession planning starts two years or more out, during which time the agency builds bench strength and disperses leadership functions and key stakeholder relationships among top managers.

Dwayne's style was to relate one-on-one with his deputies, to seek their input into major decisions erratically, and to delegate very little to them as a team. However, it was clear that this management style would not serve Main Street's future, so close attention was given to building a team culture among managers. Over the months of transition work, Dwayne gradually pulled back and eventually delegated the crafting of his final annual budget to the team.

Human resource systems and the agency's technologies were reviewed and recommendations made for needed upgrades.

Finally, all of Dwayne's key relationships with funders and school administrators were backed up either by a top deputy or by a board member.

In setting strategic directions, the board set a goal for expanding the agency's highly touted school-based academic support services. Recruitment for Dwayne's successor began six months before his departure. A dynamic woman of a younger generation was hired. She quickly solidified the internal capacity-building begun over the past two years and began pursuing funds to support the agency's expansion.

▲ ▲ ▲

Most of the nonprofits in transition that we've served could be slotted into one of the above categories. However, each of these over three hundred agencies has presented a unique constellation of organizational strengths, needs, and dynamics. Our success in assisting our clients to exploit the opportunities in their leadership transitions has been a function of how well we engage with them to identify the critical features upon which their future achievements depend.

Now that you have a better understanding of the context and framework of the executive transition process under your belt, you're ready to dive into Chapter Two, where we present an overview of the Executive Transition Management model. Soon you will be on your way to planning your organization's executive transition.

Chapter Two:
Essential Elements of a Successful Leadership Transition

▷ Chapter Two begins with an overview of the three phases of the Executive Transition Management model: Prepare, Pivot, and Thrive. These phases take an agency from the moment its executive announces her intention to resign through the first few months of the next executive's tenure. Properly executed, the phases help the organization to prepare a good ending with the departing leader and to conduct the work necessary to ensure a good beginning with the successor.

The second part of this chapter addresses the essential elements necessary to a successful leadership transition: board leadership and engagement, healthy closure with the departing executive, strategic review, staff engagement, attracting qualified candidates, screening candidates, and launching the new executive.

Through these phases and essential elements, the organization expands its perspectives on what its clients need, adds new roles, and develops new ways of thinking about how to do its work. For instance, the board leading the transition to new staff leadership must step into a new, more hands-on role, and they must engage directly with the people central to their agency's community impact. These actions ultimately bring the organization to the selection of the right new leader and to the fulfillment of community goals.

The Three Phases of Executive Transition Management

The Executive Transitions Management (ETM) protocol presented in this book is a flexible set of practices designed to help nonprofits take advantage of the renewal opportunities in their leadership transitions. Tom Adams, now president of TransitionGuides, developed the first versions of these practices in his work with members of NeighborWorks America. The author, based on his consulting history with agencies in transition, modified and expanded on Adams's work in setting up CompassPoint's Executive Transitions Management program in 1997. In 2000, with funding from the Annie E. Casey Foundation, CompassPoint and TransitionGuides of Silver Spring, Maryland, collaborated in creating the "Prepare, Pivot, and Thrive" formulation presented here. Beginning in 2004, CompassPoint, again with funding from the Casey Foundation, created a three-day training for consultants wanting to employ the model with their clients. Since then the training has been presented in several cities across the country.

The activities involved cover the entire transition process from the announcement that the current executive is leaving to the successful launch of the new leader. It combines traditional executive search techniques with organizational capacity-building work in a way that can be tailored to the needs of any agency. The result is a positive, forward-looking relationship between an executive who fits the organization's leadership needs and an organization and board that is prepared to work with this talented new leader.

Let's explore the three phases of ETM.

PREPARE: Clarify Direction and Leadership Requirements

In Phase 1, Prepare, the board seeks answers to the questions, Where are we going and what kind of leader will get us there?

Central to this first phase is an efficient process for clarifying the agency's broad strategic directions and the leadership skills needed to pursue them. A transition and search committee is appointed by the board and takes on key transition questions:

- ▷ What are our strategic directions going forward?
- ▷ What transformations should the agency make to achieve the impacts needed by our clientele?
- ▷ What do these directions and impacts say about the attributes we should seek in the next executive?
- ▷ What changes do we as a governing body need to make?
- ▷ What are the agency's operational strengths? Where do we fall short, and what are our plans for addressing the deficiencies?
- ▷ What will be expected of the executive in his first twelve to eighteen months to pursue our strategic goals and to build organizational capacity?

Additionally, the early transition needs of the agency and the departing executive are addressed in this initial phase. The organization will want to ensure an appropriate good-bye and ending for the departing executive. Would she benefit from working with a coach on how to leave in a way that serves the needs of the agency and doesn't neglect her needs? If the executive leaves before the search is completed, is there an internal person qualified to serve as "acting" executive? Or will the agency need to find external candidates for interim leadership?

If there are serious operational problems (for example, a fiscal crisis) that affect the organization's readiness to hire or that may distract the board from the search process, an agency may spend extra time in the Prepare phase to resolve issues and to stabilize operations before starting a search. In some cases, an interim executive director will be brought in to address current problems; the next permanent executive can then focus on the future. And if there are serious structural problems, putting the house in order before starting the search will make it easier to attract top-notch candidates.

PIVOT: Executive Search and Selection, Organizational Improvement, and Staff Morale

Executive Transition Management activities in this middle phase focus on three areas—executive search and selection, organizational improvement, and staff morale.

As the Pivot phase opens, the organization conducts a diligent and energetic search that recruits a diverse candidate pool whose skills match those of the candidate profile developed in the Prepare phase. Resumes are screened, the top candidates interviewed, references checked, and a new executive is chosen by the board.

A second focus is on addressing some of the organizational deficiencies identified in the scoping work of the Prepare phase—that is, spiffing up the organizational platform on which the new executive will stand. For example, the departing executive might focus on securing grants to complete the funding for the next year's operations. Other examples include catching up on delinquent financial reports or revising the chart of accounts to better fit current budgeting. Training in supervisory skills for managers could address performance and morale problems among frontline staff.

A third area of attention is on the less tangible human issues related to transition—staff morale. When an executive departure is announced, staff members experience a range of emotions from regretting the loss of the executive to uneasiness and uncertainty about the future of the agency. They need supportive reassurances that such feelings are normal. And as an antidote to their anxieties, they need clear and repeated communications about the agency's strategic directions, the candidate profile, the search process, and the capacity-building activities being undertaken.

THRIVE: Post-hire Launch and Support

In this final phase, the new executive is oriented to the agency, its strategic directions, and the board's initial performance expectations for the executive. Board and executive become a team by making explicit how each wants to be supported by the other. Similarly, the executive negotiates with the staff management group how he and they will function as a team. The executive begins meeting with the major supporters of the agency—foundation program officers, civic leaders, and major donors.

Sixty-five percent of entering executives are doing the job for the first time.[8] This means most would benefit from some form of professional learning and support to develop their executive skills, for instance, a class or certification program for picking up a missing skill, a coach or a mentor to facilitate building the fit between the new leader and the job, or a peer support group. The board initiates the discussion on skill development needs, budgets for it, and monitors the executive's progress.

After two months or so on the job, the executive sits with the board and reviews the initial performance and development goals and modifies them based on the executive's enhanced knowledge of what's realistic given time and resources available.

The Essential Elements for a Successful Transition

Chapters Three, Four, and Five present the series of steps that make up the ETM recipe for productively managing a nonprofit leadership transition. While all the steps are important, the demands may be beyond your resources, and you may well decide to cut back on the ETM recipe. Therefore, this section highlights what CompassPoint has found to be the seven essential elements necessary to a fully successful executive transition, ingredients that should not be cut out if you reduce the larger recipe. Leaving any one of them out can result, in the best case, in a bland and unsatisfactory outcome. In the worst case, the transition will fail in one or more ways: The new executive will have a short and troubled tenure, staff will leave, funders will desert the agency, or the agency's programs will become increasingly out of touch with its constituencies' needs.

Let's look at these essential ingredients that, in ten years of transition consulting, we've learned are necessary to a successful outcome.

Board Leadership and Engagement

The board has to come to the work wholeheartedly for two reasons. First, hiring the right executive is one of its most important duties. And second, there are significant opportunities for agency renewal in the transition moment. The president or the executive committee appoints an able chair and assigns members with the time and aptitudes for the transition work. The board and committee are honest about their capacities to follow the necessary steps. Where they lack the needed skills or time, they engage a coach or consultant for guidance and work capacity. They pursue the funding necessary to pay for that guidance.

As the committee does its work, the larger board steps in at two key points: setting the agency's strategic directions and picking the new executive from among the finalists. At the transition outset, the committee establishes its work plan and timeline. All board members must plan to attend the special board sessions for setting directions and for interviewing the finalists.

The board sets the tone for the entire process. Staff, funders, and constituents look to the board to model enthusiasm and diligence in planning the agency's future.

Seven Essential Ingredients

This book includes many ingredients that will help your organization enjoy a successful executive transition. Some organizations, due to time or resources, will need to cut some of the ingredients. Years of experience have taught us that the seven elements below MUST be included by all organizations to have a successful outcome.

1. Board leadership and engagement
2. Healthy closure with the departing executive director
3. Strategic review and candidate profile
4. Staff engagement
5. Attraction of qualified candidates
6. Thorough candidate screening
7. Attention to the new executive's launch

However you alter the recipe in this book, be sure that you include the seven ingredients above.

Healthy Closure with the Departing Executive Director

As stated earlier, a good beginning starts with a good ending. Central to the ending is closure with the incumbent. Chapter Three includes a section on the facets of that closure that need attention—good-bye rituals, personal and professional barriers to letting go, clear boundaries on any ongoing formal role with the agency, and others. For the long-tenured executive whose identity is tightly woven into the agency's public identity, a professional coach for the executive can be a potent and efficient resource.

Meanwhile, the board must focus on (and be excited about) the future of the agency. Simultaneously, it needs to honor the departing executive and her legacy. This can be an uncomfortable time for board and executive. The board must resist the temptation to minimize its discomfort by ignoring the closure activities. That discomfort can lead the board to procrastinate closure, because the board knows that the executive will be out the door shortly and perhaps out of sight. The ending *must* be attended to, or unresolved issues may sabotage the new beginning and new leadership.

Strategic Review and Candidate Profile

A board will know what kind of leader it needs after it knows where it's going. And the more perspectives it taps—staff, departing executive, funders, community leaders—the better its map. The strategic directions set at this point will be the source of the candidate skills profile used in the executive search and of the leadership priorities for the new executive.

Staff Engagement

Minimally, the board and its transition committee need to communicate clearly, directly, and frequently with staff as the transition and search process unfolds. Transparency about the transition process will mitigate staff uneasiness and confusion.

While transparency is essential, pulling staff into the transition and search process increases the likelihood of success. Boards should solicit staff input on strategic directions and capacity-building needs, get their feedback on the candidate profile, encourage them to recruit candidates, and give them some time with the finalists prior to the board's interviews with them. To involve staff, seat a staff liaison on the transition committee and have committee members involve staff directly at crucial points in the process, such as when assessing strengths and weaknesses in administrative systems and when identifying unmet client needs.

Attraction of Qualified Candidates

A good strategic review builds board excitement about and commitment to the agency's future. In turn, that excitement energizes the aggressive recruitment needed to uncover strong candidates. Board members who believe in their agency and who are invested in its fresh goals can better attract qualified candidates to the executive position.

The committee must develop a solid list of contacts, assign members to pursuing them, and monitor follow-through. Doing little more than posting the position on the right web sites runs the serious risk of turning up little more than a pool of lesser candidates.

Thorough Candidate Screening

Candidates must be screened against the profile of skills and characteristics that were detailed in the candidate profile. The chemistry and attractiveness of candidates as they emerge in face-to-face board interviews are important. But experienced recruiters stress that data derived in the interviews account for less than half of the information that should be gathered on a candidate.

Besides posing questions to the candidates, a board might ask them to make a presentation on a strategic topic, with advance preparation or on the spot. Going to dinner with a candidate allows for a less formal interaction and another view on a candidate. Giving staff a chance to interact with the candidates provides a source of input to the board. And most important, checking with references who can speak to what the candidate has done with past management and leadership challenges is essential.

Attention to the New Executive's Launch

A board's transition work is not complete without careful attention to setting up its new executive for a productive start. In launching the new executive, the board sets first-year performance priorities and evaluation methods. The board and the executive make explicit how they will work as a team—how each will support and challenge the other. Together, board and executive (especially a first-time executive) reflect on the skills he should develop in light of the strategic directions of the agency.

Sticking around for these final transition tasks can be a stretch for a committee that's worn down by the rigors of the Prepare and the Pivot phases of its work. In anticipation of needing a break, some committees recruit a fresh pair of board members to carry out the "thrive" activities.

▲ ▲ ▲

You now have a basic grounding in the ETM process and recommended considerations for successful transition planning. The next three chapters will focus on the individual phases of the model (Prepare, Pivot, Thrive) in greater detail and provide tools and advice you can use immediately.

Chapter Three:
Prepare

▷ This chapter addresses the first phase of the ETM model—*Prepare*. It provides detailed guidance on the steps an organization needs to execute to prepare for a successful executive transition.

The first section of the chapter focuses on creating and defining the roles and activities of the transition committee. The second section provides a framework for setting the agency's *leadership agenda,* which includes updating the vision statement, setting strategic goals in pursuit of that vision, and identifying the organizational capacity upgrades needed to pursue the goals. It also includes a first look at what the board will expect the next executive to achieve in his first twelve months toward realizing the strategic goals.

The last section of the chapter explains how to transform the results of a leadership agenda into a candidate profile for use in recruiting. With the leadership agenda and candidate profile in place, an agency maximizes its chances of securing an executive who can lead the agency to where it wants to go.

Getting Organized

"How things begin is how things end" is a statement that holds true for a board's management of a leadership transition. Careful attention to getting the work off on the right foot increases the chances of successfully hiring a new executive who fits future leadership needs.

Forming a Transition Committee

One of the primary duties of a board of directors is the hiring and monitoring of its chief executive. In that regard, it needs to devote extensive and careful attention to managing the agency's transition to new staff leadership. Some of the challenges and bumps boards often encounter in temporarily stepping up to this expanded agency leadership role are described in the article "Stepping Up: A Board's Challenge in Leadership Transition," which appears in Appendix A.

As soon as a board learns the executive position will be vacant, an ad hoc transition and search committee should be set up. The board chair appoints three to five board members. It's important that those appointed can commit the time needed for the committee's work. The typical transition committee meets about five times over a four- to five-month period. The work demands can be greater if there's more than the usual preparation work needed before the search begins, as with an agency described in Chapter One as being "in decline." If the committee will be doing the transition work without the help of a consultant, it's important that one of the committee members be experienced in managing leadership transitions.

The transition committee will oversee all the tasks essential to a successful transition in staff leadership. One of the board's officers should serve as committee chair to keep the work in sync with other board activities and connected to the leadership of the board.

Let's take a closer look at the duties of the transition committee, its chair, any staff who sit on the committee, and the departing executive.

Duties of the Transition Committee

The transition committee is responsible for the following tasks related to the transition:

1. Assure a healthy **closure with the departing executive.**

   ▶ Acknowledge the executive's achievements and legacy; create good-bye rituals.

   ▶ Provide opportunities, especially to staff, for coming to terms with the loss of their leader and for envisioning what they want in their next leader.

   ▶ Elicit executive's advice on future vision for the agency and on the successor profile.

   ▶ Transfer, as needed, the key executive duties to staff, board, and interim executive—especially financial oversight, fundraising, contracts management, and program oversight.

   ▶ Define the future role (if any) of the departing executive.

2. Plan the **transition and search activities.**

- ▸ Contract for any outside consultation needed in the transition.
- ▸ Assure involvement of staff in transition and search activities—to gain their unique perspectives and to alleviate their anxieties.
- ▸ Communicate the board's transition and search plan to all key internal and external stakeholders.
- ▸ Update the agency's future vision.
- ▸ Assess the agency's current status—strengths, challenges, opportunities.
- ▸ Attend to any serious deficits in agency systems that deserve immediate attention.
- ▸ Create the candidate profile of skills and characteristics needed in the next executive.
- ▸ Plan and execute the executive search.
- ▸ Personally contact and recruit executive candidates.
- ▸ Screen candidates, check references, and forward a list of finalists to board for selection.
- ▸ Negotiate terms of employment with selected executive.
- ▸ Appoint an interim executive if needed.

3. Assure a healthy **beginning for the new executive.**

- ▸ Orient the executive to agency programs, systems, people, and stakeholders.
- ▸ Establish solid lines of communication between board and executive.
- ▸ Delineate initial performance goals for executive.
- ▸ Create a professional development plan for executive.
- ▸ Specify performance evaluation system and evaluation dates for executive.

Duties of the Transition Committee Chair

The chair of the transition committee is a critical focal point of an agency's transition and search process. The chair of the board of directors or a member of the executive committee frequently takes on this role.

Some key responsibilities of the transition committee chair include the following:

- ▷ In consultation with the board's executive committee, recruit board and staff members to serve on the transition committee.

- ▷ Lead transition committee meetings, with support from the transition consultant, if one is engaged.

- ▷ Monitor the contracts as to deliverables and costs with any consultants engaged to assist the committee.

- ▷ Assure that the activities necessary to a "good ending" with the departing executive are carried out.

- ▷ Serve as the main liaison between the transition committee and the departing executive.

- ▷ Ensure that committee ground rules and confidentiality are observed.

- ▷ Monitor the timeline for the transition process and negotiate changes with committee members and with consultant when needed.

- ▷ Provide key support to an interim executive director if one is in place.

- ▷ Be the primary communication link to the board of directors on the activities of the transition committee.

- ▷ Act as the spokesperson to the community on the agency's transition activities.

- ▷ Support staff members on the committee in their responsibilities to communicate with the rest of staff on the transition work.

- ▷ Extend offer verbally and in writing to board's choice for executive (if authority has been given by the board of directors).

- ▷ Lead the orientation and support efforts with the new executive.

- ▷ Coordinate communication to key stakeholders on the selection of the new executive.

Staff Representation on the Transition Committee

CompassPoint typically recommends that the committee include two staff representatives, one of the top managers and one line staff. Staff inclusion has two benefits: It brings an important perspective, and it increases staff buy-in for the transition work and for the eventual hire. More than the board, staff deeply understand the internal workings of the agency and programmatic opportunities going forward. This knowledge helps the committee reach a more complete picture of what's needed in the next executive.

Hiring the executive is the board's duty. Typically staff on the committee help in three ways: They scope out current administrative needs; they help craft a future vision; and they help recruit. Less frequently, staff participate in the board's interviews with the candidates and in deliberations on whom to hire.

Staff representatives should be chosen for their ability to see the big picture in discussing the leadership needs of the agency. Caution them not to consider themselves advocates for their particular department or program. A key staff function is to serve as a two-way communications channel between staff and the transition committee, bringing staff views to committee deliberations (sometimes via surveys and interviews as described later) and keeping staff abreast of the committee's activities. The content of some of the committee discussions will need to be kept confidential, but sharing updates on the transition process serves to calm a staff anxious about the future.

As a condition of membership, board and staff members on the committee should declare that they will not seek the executive position. A committee member who later becomes a candidate taints the process either by having moved the job description in the direction of her qualifications or by creating the external perception that she did so.

Role of the Departing Executive

The question of what the departing executive's role should be in the transition and search process is a big one. On the one hand, the incumbent executive knows what it takes to do the job, understands the internal systems, and can see opportunities for new directions. On the other hand, the executive will soon be gone. Her participation might prevent the board, as the body responsible for the success of the agency, from fully owning decisions and commitments about where the agency needs to go. And those decisions may vary from what the departing executive would recommend. Some boards—especially those with strong executives—are in the habit of being led by or are reluctant to disagree with the executive.

It is best if the executive serves as on-call advisor careful to provide input but not to direct the decisions. The executive should not be a member of the committee. Steering clear of influencing the decision is one of the ways the executive lets go and helps the board take leadership. In some cases, the board has never before taken such a strong hand and may never have met without the executive. The executive's reduced influence may pain him, but it's necessary to

Tools You'll Need for Committee Meetings

Tool 1: Sample Agenda for First Meeting of the Transition Committee

Tool 2: Sample Timeline & Work Plan

Tool 3: Communications Plan: First Letter to Stakeholders

the investment the board needs to have to see the agency into its future.

Holding the First Committee Meeting

The foundation for a successful and smooth transition process is created in the first meeting of the transition committee. Time invested at the beginning to build trust and clarify structure and roles pays enormous dividends in later meetings, when tough decisions have to be made. The first step is to set norms for candid, constructive discussions. A second major task is to come to an agreement on the work to be done over the course of the transition and on how it will be accomplished.

This first meeting can require three hours or more. It's a big chunk of time, but attention to team building and to getting all the details in place now will prevent problems later that can derail or slow the committee's work. The first meeting should cover the following topics:

▶ Introductions and team building

▶ Committee process, membership, and context

▶ Duties, work plan, scheduling, and other logistics

▶ Transition budget and consulting contract

▶ Assessing leadership needs

▶ Researching executive compensation

▶ Communications plan

▶ Evaluation of meeting

Tool 1 shows how these topics can be integrated into an agenda for the first meeting of the transition committee. Let's explore each of these topics in order.

Sample Agenda for First Meeting of the Transition Committee

MISSION YOUTH SERVICES
Transition Committee

AGENDA
Organizing Meeting
November 10, 2009
5:00 p.m. to 8:30 p.m.

5:00   Introduction by chair: Welcome to the committee
5:10   Agenda review
5:20   Introductions & team building:
Team building exercise: "Hopes & Commitments"—*Members will introduce themselves, describe their hopes for the outcome of the transition process, and state what personal commitment they're making to achieving those hopes.*
6:00   Committee logistics:
- How we will operate: Ground rules   - Clerical support
- Decision-making rules   - Consultant duties
- Meeting times   - Role of departing executive
- Roster & contact information
6:40   BREAK
6:50   What are the big competing activities—November 2009 to June 2010:
- Creation and board adoption of the annual budget (January to December fiscal year)
- The board-produced holiday dinner for clients
- The annual spring fundraising gala
- Other
7:00   Mapping the transition—work plan & timeline**:
- Interim executive *(if needed)*
        Profile
        Selection process
- Transition & search
        Acknowledging the departing executive
        Organizational assessment
        Strategic review & leadership planning
        Recruit
        Screen
        Hire
- New executive installation
7:50   Stakeholder communications plan
8:00   Next steps:
- Review assignments
- Set next meeting date
8:15   Meeting evaluation *(What worked well & what would we change to make for a better meeting next time?)*
8:30   ADJOURN

** Ideally the committee chair will have created the first draft of a work plan and timeline and sent it to the members prior to the meeting. These documents are modified in the meeting based on members' input.

Introductions and Team Building

The makeup of a transition committee varies tremendously from one organization to the next. In some cases, members all know each other well, and little effort is spent on introductions and developing trust. In other situations, members are meeting each other for the first time, and the group will need to work to become a team. Begin by taking time to make introductions, including background and experience with transitions.

The committee will be doing important and sometimes tough work. Consider offering a team-building activity in the first meeting, especially if members are not already well acquainted. For instance, staff on the committee may be unknown to board members. One "warm-up" exercise is to have each committee member, in introducing himself, tell how he came to his current role with the agency. A second exercise has each member speak to her vision of an ideal outcome to the committee's work and to what she is personally committing to do to reach that outcome.

Committee Process, Membership, and Context

The group needs to know the process it will use, how it will make decisions, and the limits on its power. Members need to review what their various roles are. For example, staff members have a duty to represent all staff and to communicate back to staff. Board members have a similar duty with the board and ultimately are also responsible for hiring the executive. If other community members are involved, their role should also be discussed.

After clarifying roles, the committee should address the rules that will help it to reach good outcomes in an efficient manner. A few explicit ground rules are helpful toward keeping discussions constructive and inclusive of all members, avoiding dominance by any one member. Some typical ground rules include the following:

▸ Confidentiality—what's said in committee stays in committee except for what the committee agrees will be communicated out.

▸ Share the air—those members who tend to be more generous with their comments need to step back regularly to make space for those less quick to speak up.

▸ It's okay to think out loud—there are no dumb thoughts or questions.

In addition, the committee needs to decide how it will make decisions. Is the goal to reach consensus? When consensus is not reached, will the decision be put to committee vote? Will staff members on the committee have a vote? With regard to the transition work, note that board members have a duty beyond that of other committee members. Remind non-board committee members that setting future directions for the agency and choosing the next executive director are ultimately the job of the board. Operating from that perspective, boards, while making clear they need and want staff and community input, must assert their final authority in committee decisions. The position of the board members prevails when decisions cannot be reached by consensus.

Review the organization's current context—any major agency activities that are competing for time and resources (for example, major fundraising drives, introduction of new systems), relevant timing issues (for example, summer activities or winter holidays) that could disrupt work, and so forth.

Committee Duties, Work Plan, Scheduling, and Logistics

At this time, the chair should also cover the duties of the group, described earlier in this chapter (see page 32). Those duties drive the content of the work plan, which drives the schedule. The full transition work plan will cover all the steps essential to a successful outcome (the activities described in the section on transition committee duties). Tool 2 provides a sample preliminary timeline and work plan for a transition and search process that you can adapt to the activities and anticipated time needs of your committee. The work plan (to the degree it has been mapped out) will need to be reviewed as part of the first meeting. The chair should sketch a basic work plan prior to the meeting and set basic deadlines. These can be revised as the work of the committee ensues.

It's best to set tentative dates for all the committee meetings within the timeline *at the first meeting*. Often the most challenging task in this first meeting is finding dates that fit into the members' personal schedules. Be sure to ask all members to bring their calendars to the meeting!

In addition to scheduling, the committee should decide how to fulfill its logistical needs. For example, the chair's duty is to organize and facilitate meetings (or to see that this is done). Someone should be appointed to handle business such as scheduling the meeting place, arranging beverages and food when needed, keeping a roster of contact information, and tracking communications among members. Another person should be appointed to keep and distribute minutes, record decisions, and note assigned tasks. If additional clerical support will be needed, the committee should identify who will seek or provide it.

Sample Timeline & Work Plan

MISSION YOUTH SERVICES
Executive Transition: Preliminary Timeline

Date	Meetings and Activities	Who
Nov. 10	**Transition committee meeting** • Get organized • Plan search for interim executive—for January 4 start date • Outline agency assessment activities and assign subcommittee to carry them out • Assign executive acknowledgment rituals to subcommittee	Committee members
Week of Nov. 16	**Activities** • Start agency scan: interviews & surveys • Begin interim executive recruitment	Assessment subcommittee Committee chair
Week of Nov. 23	*HAPPY THANKSGIVING!*	
Nov. 30	**Transition committee meeting** • Interview interim executive candidates • Forward name of chosen candidate to board for interview and hire	Committee members Committee chair
Week of Dec. 7	**Activities** • Analyze data from agency assessment	Assessment subcommittee

Dec. 14	**Transition committee meeting**
	• Review assessment data
	• Create first draft of leadership agenda:
	  ○ Major issues & challenges for Mission Youth Services
	  ○ Future vision & strategic directions
	  ○ Organizational upgrades needed
	• Craft profile of ideal executive candidate
	• Review subcommittee report on executive acknowledgment rituals
		Committee members

Weeks of Dec. 21, Jan. 4, and Jan. 11	**Activities** • Write up the leadership agenda • Draft position announcement for executive recruiting that incorporates the candidate profile	Assessment subcommittee
HAPPY HOLIDAYS!		
Jan. 4	Interim executive begins work	

Jan. 11	**Transition committee meeting** • Finalize leadership agenda • Review organizational upgrades needed—what starts now in the Pivot phase and what will wait for the new executive in the Thrive phase • Finalize candidate profile • Finalize position announcement for recruiting • Set executive search plans	Committee members
Week of Jan. 18	Begin executive candidate recruitment	*Carried as assigned by committee members*
February	Recruitment continues	
March	**Transition committee meeting—***late month* • Review resumes • Choose 6 to 8 first-round interviewees	Committee members
April	**Transition committee meeting—***mid-month* • Interview first-round candidates • Choose 2 to 3 finalists for board screening • Check references on finalists	Committee members
May	**Finalists' interviews with staff and interim executive** **Board meeting—Interview finalists and make a choice** **Transition committee meeting—***late month* • Plan entry of new executive • Script the *Thrive* activities that will be carried out by the board executive committee • Evaluate the transition/search process • Celebrate a job well done	Staff and interim executive Board of directors Committee members
June	**New executive director begins work** **Executive meets with board committee to discuss *Thrive* activities**	Board executive committee Executive director

NOTES

• This work plan and timeline was crafted by the committee chair *prior* to the first meeting of the transition committee on November 10. It was based on discussions with the board executive committee. It was presented to the committee for their review and changes. Dates were then chosen for meetings through January.
• If the board has hired a consultant to work with them through the transition, the consultant will likely carry out most of the work that occurs between meetings in the above work plan. There will be no subcommittees.

Transition Budget and Consulting Contract

With the major work pieces outlined, the committee will need to project its expenses and identify the revenues to cover them. It will speed the committee's budgeting work if the chair has drafted a proposed budget *before* the meeting (perhaps in consultation with the executive) and sent it to the committee in advance of the first meeting. Basic costs to be considered are

▸ Any direct committee expenses such as food and travel costs (for national boards)

▸ Recruitment expenses such as print and electronic advertising and long-distance phone charges

▸ Candidate travel costs, if the committee decides to partially or fully cover them

Agencies that are able to fundraise for transition and search costs might also budget for

▸ Staff time spent on committee work

▸ Hours the departing executive devotes to advising the committee, orienting the new executive, and consulting to the incoming executive over the first few months

▸ Relocation subsidy for the new executive

The largest potential expense is a contract with a transition and search consultant. The decision on whether one is needed will likely have been made by the board or its executive committee before the work of the committee has begun.[9] If one has been brought on, she will have begun planning with the committee chair prior to this first meeting and will play a guiding role in the meeting. Review the contract deliverables with the committee to ensure that everyone understands what is expected of the consultant and what the consultant expects of the committee.

Assessing Leadership Needs

The committee will be gathering input from various sources as it assesses what the organization needs from its next leader. At this first meeting, the committee discusses the processes it will use—how members want the assessment conducted, who will do it, and how the information will be fed back to the committee. Assessments will need to be made of the agency's strategic directions, of the gaps that need to be addressed to successfully pursue those goals, and of the leadership and management skills the next executive needs to be able to resolve the gaps and reach the goals.[10]

Researching Executive Compensation

The committee will need to research salary and benefits packages for executives of comparable agencies before recruiting begins in the Pivot phase. In this first meeting, find a committee member or members to take on that task.

If you suspect the current executive's salary has fallen significantly below market rates for his position, the chair will need to plan time to engage the board's executive committee in adjusting the salary range for the next executive and in planning for possible raises for other managers. The transition committee will likely need full board approval of any significant jumps in the top salary.

Setting a significantly higher salary for the next executive can sour the "ending" with the departing executive and leave the board and staff uneasy because of the disparity. The board might consider giving the departing executive a special exit compensation package, depending on the circumstances of the departure. For a longtime leader who is retiring after a successful tenure, some special compensation seems well deserved. At the other end of the spectrum, for the shorter-term executive leaving for a higher-paying job, an exit package seems less necessary for a "good ending."

Communications Plan

Communications with stakeholder groups is a critical task of the committee. Clients, funders, donors, and staff are looking for reassurance that the board is taking a strong hand in managing the transition to a new executive. Constituents feel unsettled on learning a leader is leaving. Funders can pull back, donors can leave, and staff morale can suffer.

The committee can largely mitigate the unsettledness by publicizing details of the transition plan. They must communicate to stakeholders that the board is energetically stepping up to lead the agency through a thoughtful transition process, one that will look to build on the departing leader's legacy by updating strategies to have even greater community impact.

Gathering Salary Data

The availability of data on nonprofit salaries varies from community to community. There may be a foundation or nonprofit organization that conducts an annual salary and benefits survey in your region. The local United Way may track salaries. A less immediate source is Guidestar.org. GuideStar is a national database on nonprofit organizations; its data include the 990s that all 501(c)(3) organizations are required to file with the Internal Revenue Service (IRS). The top five salaries paid by the agency are listed on an organization's 990. Information can also be collected by calling local agencies comparable in size and type of service to your agency.

Prior to the meeting, the chair, or her designee, should meet with the executive director and draft a communications plan for committee consideration and adoption. The executive will have the best grasp of the key agency stakeholders with whom the committee should communicate: government and foundation funders, major donors, community partners, staff, and volunteers. The plan should name them and specify who will contact them and how.

For example, the committee chair and executive directors might phone key funders and send a personal message to major donors. A letter from the board chair can be placed in the next agency newsletter. A committee member might attend the next all-staff meeting to present the transition work plan and to describe how staff will contribute to the agency assessment and candidate selection process. The communications role of staff members on the committee can be highlighted.

Tool 3 is a sample letter you can adapt to send out following the first committee meeting. It serves to communicate that the board has thoughtfully stepped up to its leadership responsibilities and emphasizes the forward-looking nature of the committee's transition work.

Evaluation of Meeting

Evaluate the meeting at its close for what worked and what didn't work. This helps ensure a productive committee process. Use the results to plan the next meeting.

Updating the Agency's Leadership Agenda

Tools for Strategic Direction and Leadership Agenda

Tool 4: Board Survey Questions

Tool 5: Board Self-Assessment Survey

Tool 6: Sample Staff Survey

Tool 7: Sample Questions for Community Interviews

Tool 8: Creating the Leadership Agenda

Tool 9: Sample Leadership Agenda

Tool 10: Sample Candidate Profile

Overview

Hiring an executive director before clarifying the strategic directions is like filling a plane with passengers and fuel and then telling the pilot to take them where he wants to.

A best practice in any enterprise is to work from a strategic plan. Having clarity about the community impacts your nonprofit agency seeks to achieve helps you to do a better job of getting the right talents in place and of spending on the right activities. To know what skills you need in your next executive, you first need to know what the agency seeks

Communications Plan: First Letter to Stakeholders

November 25, 2009

Dear Supporter,

I am writing to announce an important leadership transition at Mission Youth Services. Over the past year the board of directors and Lincoln Chiu, our executive director, have been discussing how to best allow Lincoln to take a long-deserved rest and to bring on new leadership.

We would like to let you know that Lincoln Chiu will step down from the executive director's position in January 2010. Lincoln will take time to rest but will continue working with Mission Youth Services on special projects and to facilitate a smooth transition over the coming year.

The agency is in a good position as we move into next year, and we want to take our time in finding a new executive director. A transition committee chaired by Eric Pineda of our board will work with staff and CompassPoint Nonprofit Services to bring in an interim executive director from its excellent Executive Transitions Management program. With the help of a seasoned temporary executive from this program as well as the active involvement of the board and staff, we look forward to Mission Youth Services continuing its excellent work with all of you.

While we will not be saying good-bye to Lincoln Chiu right away, we do want to acknowledge the wonderful leadership that he has provided over the last twelve years. He plans to continue to be actively involved in the community and will take this opportunity to rest and reflect. Lincoln has done a wonderful job in providing a vision and bringing in excellent managers to carry on the work. He will leave behind a legacy of spirited service and leadership to our community.

Early next year we will begin our search for a new permanent executive director. At that time we will send you the formal job announcement. I encourage you to send us the names of persons you think would be good candidates for our executive director position.

On behalf of the board and staff, I thank you for all the support and encouragement you have given over the years to Mission Youth Services, to Lincoln Chiu, and to the people we serve. We trust this important partnership will continue and grow during our transition and well into the future.

Sincerely,

Betsy Wilson
Chair, Board of Directors

to accomplish in the next three to five years and what building of agency capabilities is needed to make those goals possible. For instance, the skill set needed by an executive charged with opening agency outposts in neighboring counties is different from that of the leader asked to update a client service model that is out of date and losing funders.

If the agency has completed a strategic plan recently (within the past twelve months), the transition committee will likely need to spend only a little time on clarifying strategic directions. If there is not a current set of directions in place, the committee will need to gather information to craft strategic goals that will inform the candidate profile.

Gathering Input

This assessment work is similar to the first stages of a strategic planning process. Information is gathered from key stakeholders regarding client needs, program adjustments recommended to meet those needs, and revenue sources to support the work. After seeing what's needed and what's possible in the current funding environment, the committee creates a leadership agenda that includes an updated vision and broad-brush strategies for pursuing that vision. It then presents the agenda to the board for ratification.

Five segments of the agency's stakeholders should be tapped: board, departing executive, staff, funders, and peer agencies. Some committees may also want to check in with clients on their satisfaction with services and for ideas on services to be added. There may be other important audiences for some agencies, such as a volunteer corps that's essential to the agency's operations.

The Board

As the body ultimately responsible for the agency's mission and achievements, the board will review and ratify the strategic goals derived from questions placed to stakeholders. However, it's helpful to tap board perspectives prior to their hearing from others. A sample set of questions is provided in Tool 4, Board Survey Questions, page 47. The transition committee will gather, tabulate, and merge the responses with the perspectives from other sources.

The board also should be asked to assess how well it's carrying out its governance duties. Important to the agency's success going forward with a new executive is a high-performing board that shares leadership with the executive. Tool 5 is a sample Board Self-Assessment Survey that provides a template you can use and adapt to your agency. Consider making this survey available online for easier administration and faster turnaround. Note: The executive director (and other staff who frequently work with the board) also might be asked to fill out this survey. A comparison of the results with board responses could provide a broader view on board functioning.

Board responses are tabulated by a transition committee member. The results should be discussed in a board meeting and the board asked to set priorities for improving its performance. If the board needs major development work, the next executive's skills profile may need to include board-building experience.

Asking a board the question, What do you need to do to be worthy of the leadership you seek in the next executive? puts the board's self-examination in context. The agency is in transition. It is looking to retool itself to better pursue its mission. Given the emerging strategic directions, does the board need to bring new skills onto the board? Should there be greater demographic diversity among the members? Will the board need to up its ability to fundraise, for example, to pursue major donors?

TOOL 1 2 3 **4** 5 6 7 8 9 10 11 12 13 14 15 16 17 18 19 20 21 22 23 24 25 26 27 28

Board Survey Questions

The following questions are suggested as a means of getting input from board members regarding strategic directions and capacity-building needs for your agency.

1. What aspects of the current work of our agency most excite you?

2. Which of our programs do you believe are the most important to our clientele?

3. For which currently unaddressed needs of our clientele should we be looking to build programs?

4. What changes to administrative systems would improve our ability to achieve our mission?

5. What additional changes in our operations would improve services?

6. What would you consider the most significant achievements of our outgoing executive director?

7. What skill or attributes of our current executive should we pursue in the candidates to succeed her?

8. Given the unaddressed client needs and administrative improvements you cited above, what would you consider the top skills the next executive director should have?

Board Self-Assessment Survey

NS – Not satisfied
SS – Somewhat satisfied
S – Satisfied

How satisfied are you that the board
VS – Very satisfied

1. Understands the mission and purpose of the organization?   NS   SS   S   VS
2. Ensures legal compliance with federal, state, and local regulations?   NS   SS   S   VS
3. Ensures that government contract obligations are fulfilled?   NS   SS   S   VS
4. Has a strategic vision for the organization?   NS   SS   S   VS
5. Is knowledgeable about the organization's programs and services?   NS   SS   S   VS
6. Monitors the executive's performance on a regular basis?   NS   SS   S   VS
7. Provides financial oversight, including adopting a good budget?   NS   SS   S   VS
8. Monitors financial performance and projections regularly?   NS   SS   S   VS
9. Has adopted a fundraising strategy to ensure adequate resources?   NS   SS   S   VS
10. Has clear policy on fundraising responsibilities of board members?   NS   SS   S   VS
11. Acts as ambassadors to the community for the organization and its clients?   NS   SS   S   VS
12. Understands the role volunteers play at the organization?   NS   SS   S   VS
13. Understands the organization's philosophy of volunteer management?   NS   SS   S   VS
14. Understands the respective roles of the board and staff?   NS   SS   S   VS
15. Currently contains an appropriate range of expertise and diversity to make it an effective governing body?   NS   SS   S   VS
16. Effectively involves all members in board activities and responsibilities?   NS   SS   S   VS
17. Regularly assesses its own work?   NS   SS   S   VS

Scoring (NS = 1, VS = 4)

To score, add the numeric value of the response for each question and divide by the number of respondents. For example, if on question one, six board members provided answers of 1, 3, 4, 4, 2, and 2, the score for this question is **(1+3+4+4+2+2)/6, or 2.7.**

The Departing Executive

The incumbent executive will have the broadest perspective on service opportunities going forward and on the internal capacity-building needed. How and when to gather the departing executive's input varies across transitioning agencies. Some committees will include the executive as a non-voting advisor in all meetings related to setting the leadership agenda. In such cases, the executive comments on the input received from various sources and includes her own comments as well. Other committees, wary of being unduly influenced by the incumbent, will assign a committee member or two to interview the executive and bring the input to the committee meeting. The executive may also be asked to comment on the committee's draft leadership agenda before it goes to the board for possible revisions and ratification.

Staff

A staff survey frequently is used to gain staff perspectives on future goals, internal capacity needs, and the leadership profile of the next executive. To promote greater candor, survey responses are kept anonymous. Tool 6 is a Sample Staff Survey you can use as a template for your organization.

The survey attempts to balance staff input on what's right with the agency and the current executive with expressions of what they think needs to change. Any agency at any time will have room for improvements in how it delivers program. In the nonprofit world, where funding for administrative systems like human resources management and technology support is often hard to come by, requests and complaints about infrastructure tend to dominate staff responses.

Of particular interest to the committee are the questions about what changes in the agency would make for better staff performance and program outcomes. Capacity needs identified by a quarter or more of staff get attention. For instance, if "I'm getting lousy supervision" is stated by four of sixteen staff, the committee will want to follow up and explore the dimensions of the supervision problem.

The follow-up exploration of capacity needs is best done via staff group interviews conducted by someone other than a board member. This is because when board members discuss internal functions with staff members, the board undercuts managers. If there's a consultant working with the committee, he will do the follow-up. If there is staff on the transition and search committee, they can conduct the group interviews. Whether the follow-up is done by a consultant or staff member, the results should be summarized and taken *first* to the agency management team for discussion and resolution. After that, the committee should get a report on the issues raised by staff and on management's plans for addressing them.

TOOL 1 2 3 4 5 **6** 7 8 9 10 11 12 13 14 15 16 17 18 19 20 21 22 23 24 25 26 27 28

Sample Staff Survey

The transition committee seeks your help in determining what skills we should look for in the next executive director of Mission Youth Services. Staff responses to this survey will be used to

- ▶ Draft the profile of skills and attributes the board will use in recruiting candidates for executive director
- ▶ Set future directions and priorities to be addressed with the new executive

Your responses will be anonymous.

Please complete the survey by December 1. A committee member will meet with staff as a group after December 1 to report the survey results and gain more input on future directions for the agency.

To complete the survey, please go to: *(link to online survey)*

Thank you for your help!

A. What do you perceive as three of the departing executive's greatest achievements during his tenure as executive director?

1.

2.

3.

B. What elements of his leadership style as executive director do you most appreciate and would like to see carried forward by his successor?

C. What are *your* top three on-the-job achievements over the past 12 months? *(Future planning involves assessing capabilities throughout the organization, so we're interested in having individual staff members' views on their own recent successes.)*

1.

2.

3.

Community Interviews: Funders and Peer Agencies

While board and staff members are likely to be internally focused and limited in their perspective to the programs of your one agency, the program officers in the foundations and government agencies that fund your work will have a much broader view of the particular fields of service in which you operate. The

D. What three changes at the agency would most help you to be more effective *in your specific job? (Your responses are important to identifying agency improvements that would help us be more effective in serving our clients.)*

    1.

    2.

    3.

E. What three changes at the agency would help the larger agency to be more effective in pursuing its mission?

    1.

    2.

    3.

F. What three skills or capabilities do you bring to your job that especially contribute to our agency meeting its goals?

    1.

    2.

    3.

G. What are the top three skills that the next executive director will need to have in order to be successful?

    1.

    2.

    3.

H. Additional comments:

Thank you for your help!

foundation that funds a youth development agency will know about recent innovations in youth development work and about how shifting revenue streams might be threats to financial viability or might provide opportunities for program expansion.

Your agency managers can provide the names and contact information for your primary funders. Committee members can spread the calls among them. One member should take the task of gathering all the interview results into a unified report.

Besides being an important source of information for setting strategic directions, the interviews also serve to reassure funders that the board is competently managing the transition. Funders are generally flattered to be asked their opinions and appreciate the opportunity to connect with a board member.

TOOL 1 2 3 4 5 6 **7** 8 9 10 11 12 13 14 15 16 17 18 19 20 21 22 23 24 25 26 27 28

Sample Questions for Community Interviews

1. How long have you been aware of Mission Youth Services and in what capacity have you worked with the organization?

2. What do you think the purpose of Mission Youth Services is in the community?

3. What do you think are the greatest strengths of Mission Youth Services in fulfilling its purpose?

4. What do you perceive as the greatest area for possible improvement?

5. How well does Mission Youth Services collaborate with other agencies in the community?

6. What major issues do you see on the horizon that might impact (be a barrier to) Mission Youth Services successfully providing its services?

7. How do you see Mission Youth Services needing to change to meet these barriers and challenges?

8. Do you see any opportunities in the community that Mission Youth Services is missing out on and should be taking advantage of?

9. *A summary question, such as:* What do you think the highest priorities of Mission Youth Services' leadership should be in the future?

Another perspective is that of agencies doing work similar to yours and those with whom you are teamed up on a project. They can speak to their perceptions of your agency's strengths and areas needing improvement. Ask them how well you collaborate in joint efforts. They'll also have ideas on programmatic and funding trends in your agency's field.

As with identifying funders, agency staff can provide names and contact information. Members can divvy up the calls.

Volunteers and Clients

Gathering input from the first five sources is major work. Volunteers and clients usually are tapped only when the committee has outside consultants who can devote the time and expertise to do it. An exception is agencies for which a major portion of their work is carried out by volunteers, such as a food delivery program for the homebound. In those cases the committee should consider including a member of their volunteer corps on the committee. That member can then gather perspectives on strategic directions and capacity needs from his volunteer peers.

For client input, the committee might review recent client satisfaction surveys, if the agency routinely collects them. If this is not a current practice, instituting a method for gathering client evaluations might be a task assigned to the next executive.

It takes a lot of time to survey clients on how agency services could be modified or augmented to better meet their needs. As an alternative to the labor-intensive survey work, staff might be asked to present recently published reports in your service field on emerging trends in client needs and service modalities.

Arriving at the Leadership Agenda

After gathering information from multiple perspectives, the committee should devote a meeting to analyzing the data and arriving at

▶ A vision for what they'd like the agency to look like in three to five years

▶ A set of strategic directions that flow from that vision

▶ The improvements to program and administrative systems needed to pursue the strategic directions

▶ The board development needs

▶ The resulting first-year performance priorities for the next executive

The vision, strategic directions, capacity-building needs, board development plan, and executive priorities comprise the *leadership agenda.* The leadership agenda will inform what kind of leader the agency needs going forward and the candidate profile to be used in recruiting.

Tool 8 provides an overview of suggested steps the committee can take to arrive at the leadership agenda. Step 1, Gather Data, lists the sources of committee input described above. Step 2, Analyze Data, provides a set of categories for analyzing the input. Step 3 describes the process of creating the actual leadership agenda.

The process of arriving at the leadership agenda can be as simple or as expansive as the committee has the time and ability to undertake. Bottom line, the committee needs to arrive at a set of strategic directions for the agency and to identify improvements to administrative and program systems deemed necessary to pursue the strategic directions. The strategic directions need to be grounded in a review of current and unmet client needs and an industry scan of program innovations and revenue trends. In setting goals for improving the capacity of agency systems, the committee should consider which goals might be undertaken during the Pivot phase and which will be taken up by the next executive in the Thrive phase.

The executive performance priorities flow from the strategic directions and the capacity upgrades that are identified as necessary for growing the agency's community impact. To provide clear benchmarks for gauging progress toward the future vision, the priorities are stated in measurable terms. For example, *the executive will oversee the addition of two tutoring sites, a 50 percent increase in the number of private donors, and two new grants.*

If, based on the review, the committee decides that little change in program and operations is needed, the profile of the next executive may look very similar to the incumbent's skills and style. If major new directions or program modifications are called for, the skills needed to lead those changes need to be identified and given priority in screening candidates.

One or two committee members need to take the lead in preparing for and facilitating the committee's discussion and deliberations that will produce the leadership agenda. Sending advance copies of the data analysis to the committee will be important to preparing members for a productive discussion. Additional advance work might include asking the members, based on the data analysis, to propose three strategic directions for the agency and to identify the top five organizational capacity-building needs related to those aspirations.

Creating the Leadership Agenda and Candidate Profile

STEP 1: GATHER DATA

Sources of input
- Staff
- Board
- Current executive
- Funders
- Peer organizations
- Other

↓

STEP 2: ANALYZE DATA

Analyze findings from these perspectives
- Organization strengths and achievements
- Administrative and program systems capacity needs
- Unmet client needs
- Industry scan
  - Emerging program innovations
  - Revenue trends

↓

STEP 3: DEFINE THE LEADERSHIP AGENDA

Define *vision* for the organization—its aspirations for improved client and community impact over the next three to five years

↓

Set strategic directions (as informed by vision)

↓ ↓

Specify board development changes needed to achieve strategic directions	Specify programmatic and administrative capacity changes needed to achieve strategic directions

↓ ↓

Schedule the changes to be addressed as either priority upgrades during the Pivot phase
or
upgrades the new executive will take on as priorities in the Thrive phase

↓

STEP 4: ESTABLISH PERFORMANCE PRIORITIES

Based on the results of Step 3, establish performance priorities for the new executive (presented to the newly hired executive in the Thrive phase)

↓

STEP 5: CREATE CANDIDATE PROFILE

Identify the following profile requirements needed in the new executive
- Skills
- Experience
- Attributes

The meeting then focuses on comparing the directions and capacity needs each committee member identified, discussing them, and arriving at a consensus of the top directions and goals for the agency.

These are big issues; arriving at decisions will be complex. Some committees find it helpful to bring in a skilled facilitator for the meeting. Bringing in a facilitator also frees up all committee members to participate fully, rather than forcing one or two to serve in a neutral facilitation role.

After the committee arrives at a leadership agenda, it presents it, along with the supporting data analysis, to the full board for comments and suggested

TOOL 1 2 3 4 5 6 7 8 **9** 10 11 12 13 14 15 16 17 18 19 20 21 22 23 24 25 26 27 28

Sample Leadership Agenda

MISSION YOUTH SERVICES

Vision

Mission Youth Services will expand on its highly regarded academic support programs and will have a successful youth empowerment program that trains neighborhood adolescents in methods for solving community problems.

Strategic directions

- Expand the current two-site after-school tutoring program into additional school-based sites.
- Grow the youth organizing program from its currently small corps of teenagers addressing one community issue to one with a much larger enrollment of teenagers organized to advocate for solutions to a broader array of neighborhood problems.
- Increase Mission community representation on the board of directors; that is, move the board membership closer to representing the demographic diversity of the Mission neighborhood.
- Increase program revenues from private donor sources.

Pivot phase capacity upgrades

- Arrange for an orientation of entire Mission Youth Services staff and board to the concepts underpinning a youth empowerment program and to program examples from other youth development agencies.
- Compile into the agency's current database all the existing information held by the executive director and board members on donors to Mission Youth Services over the past five years.
- Research potential sources of foundation grants for the proposed Mission Youth Services youth empowerment program.
- Document the agency's procedures for recruiting, orienting, deploying, and retaining volunteer tutors who serve in Mission Youth Services' after-school tutoring program.

changes. Again, solid facilitation will be helpful in moving the board to consensus on the agenda. It's critically important that the board "own" the agenda through having fully discussed it, tweaked it, and taken a ratification vote.

The leadership agenda is the agency's road map into the future. The agency has taken stock of its past achievements, has looked at the needs of its clientele, and has set out goals for how it wants to "transform" itself to better address the needs of its clientele. The board needs to fully embrace the leadership agenda in order for the next executive and staff to successfully move the agency in the appropriate directions.

Capacity upgrades to be taken on by the new executive director

- Identify and install a fundraising software product for tracking private donors; transfer existing donor information to the new system.
- Support the board's executive committee in setting up a plan to increase the demographic diversity of the board.
- Look to remodel the agency's current administrative workspace, or to move the offices, to create a more efficient and productive work environment.
- Build the grant-writing skills of the current development associate so as to reduce the grant-writing demands on the executive position.

Board development needs

- Create a board recruitment plan with goals to increase representation from the neighborhoods served by the programs of Mission Youth Services, to expand the demographic diversity of the board, and to bring on fundraising expertise.
- Create mechanisms that will support the participation on the board of lower-income parents of program youth; for example, the provision of child care resources while parents are doing board work.
- Make board meetings more productive and rewarding for members; consider coaching on how to run productive meetings.

First-year performance priorities for the new executive

- Open a Mission Youth Services after-school tutoring program in two additional public schools.
- Convert the "youth organizing program" into a "youth empowerment department" at Mission Youth Services that has at least twenty-five youth enrolled who are beginning to address two local community needs.
- Acquire grants from at least two new foundations to support the youth empowerment department.
- Increase the number of private individual donors to Mission Youth Services by 50 percent.
- Raise the visibility of Mission Youth Services' programs with the government officials representing the neighborhoods of Mission Youth Services.

Creating the Candidate Profile

With the leadership agenda in hand, the transition and search committee next crafts a candidate profile. This profile expresses the skills, experience, and attributes that the next executive must have to successfully pursue the strategic directions and capacity-building priorities detailed in the leadership agenda.

For instance, if an agency managing a homeless shelter envisions adding a group home as a transitional housing facility to move clients permanently off the streets, what skills are needed of the leader who will create that new program? An agency that wants to dramatically cut the proportion of its revenues that comes from the government will probably seek a leader with a strong track record in fundraising. An after-school tutoring program in a low-income community that seeks to engage teens in a new leadership program focused on addressing neighborhood problems will create a profile that includes experience in community organizing and youth development. And the community health clinic that is straining to keep up with a client population that has doubled in size over the past three years needs an executive who will build systems that can handle a burgeoning caseload.

A committee will typically generate a fairly lengthy and expansive list of skills. On first blush it looks as if the next executive will be expected to be able to do it all (including walking on water). To get real and focus the recruitment on the candidates with the skills most critical to your agency, the committee needs to prioritize the skills sought. What are the top four or five, the "must-haves"? The remaining skills become preferences below the required five. The preferred skills are the add-ons that will help a candidate stand out in the group of applicants with only the required skills.

In arriving at the must-haves, it's important to consider what skills can be covered by other managers. For the homeless shelter mentioned above, maybe the director of programs has the experience needed to develop the new transitional shelter. If so, the executive's job will be to raise funds for it. Or the community health clinic might consider creating a deputy for operations position and hiring someone into it with experience in systems management in large and growing client service agencies. In this case, the executive will need to focus on current and future trends in health care delivery and on relations with major funders and neighborhood leaders.

Care must be taken to avoid setting the experience bar too high in any one skill area. Requiring ten years of top management experience rather than five years eliminates a large swath of folks who might be great for your job. Similarly, requiring an advanced college degree trims the pool dramatically. The bars should be set lower unless it can be documented that the higher bars are essential to succeeding in the job. Some of the higher bars will eliminate younger, high-aptitude talent or those who, for economic reasons, have not had access to graduate school.

Beyond its utility in focusing the recruitment activities, the profile, with skills sorted between required and preferred, will ease the committee's work of selecting candidates during the screening process. Without agreement up front on the priority skills, the committee will struggle when choosing among strong candidates with disparate profiles.

The Candidate Profile in Tool 10 (on page 60) shows a sample profile generated from the leadership agenda.

▲ ▲ ▲

In this chapter, you have learned how to move your organization through the first phase of executive transition, Prepare. In this phase, the organization readied itself for transition over the course of several weeks. It assembled a broadly representative transition committee, which became a successful team, making critical decisions and affirming them with the full board. The team's most important work product has been of two parts. First, the team assembled a well-informed picture of the agency's future direction, with special attention to the type of leadership required to make that future a reality—its leadership agenda. And second, the team translated that leadership agenda into a description of the characteristics of executive director candidates suited to the organization's goals, staff, board, and community—the candidate profile.

With these key preparation pieces in place, the agency can turn to recruiting, interviewing, and selecting its next executive—the Pivot stage.

Candidate Profile

MISSION YOUTH SERVICES

Attributes

▶ Demonstrated commitment to our core youth development mission: to build the academic skills of young people and to give them skills for improving the quality of life in their community.

▶ A deep understanding of the challenges faced by low-income, urban communities.

▶ An aptitude for bringing together diverse people and ideas to create collaborative projects.

▶ A visionary entrepreneur who has taken nonprofit agencies into new arenas.

▶ A charismatic person of energy and vitality who can motivate staff to achieve their personal best.

Skills and Experience

▶ Required

  ▶ Five years' experience in a senior management position in a community-based nonprofit agency, including budget development and financial management.

  ▶ Three years' experience in some form of youth development work or inner-city community organizing.

  ▶ Significant experience working collaboratively with persons of diverse racial and ethnic backgrounds, socioeconomic statuses, ages, and sexual orientations.

  ▶ Record of successful fundraising from public and private sources to support nonprofit agencies.

  ▶ Excellent written and oral communication skills.

  ▶ Bachelor's degree.

▶ Desirable

  ▶ History of having led organizational growth, facilitating higher levels of mission achievement. Skills include strategic planning and management of complex internal operations and external relations.

  ▶ Experience in community organizing with youth and young adults.

  ▶ Experience and familiarity with the needs and institutions of the Mission district that Mission Youth Services serves—or nonprofit work experience in a similar inner-city environment.

  ▶ Experience with the government and foundation funders of Mission Youth Services.

  ▶ Fluency in Spanish and/or in relevant Asian languages.

Chapter Four:
Pivot

> This chapter provides a comprehensive presentation of all aspects of the search and selection process. We begin with a discussion of the internal organizational capacity-building that we suggest agencies pay attention to during their transition. This is followed by detailed step-by-step guidance on the candidate search, screening, and hiring process.

Upgrading Organizational Capacity

In the Prepare phase of executive transition, the organization assembled a transition committee, assessed its strategic directions, and determined what type of leadership and candidate could best pursue those directions. The Pivot phase of executive transition begins with work on the improvements to systems and programs that were outlined for immediate attention in the leadership agenda at the culmination of the Prepare phase.

The upgrades are undertaken simultaneously with the candidate recruitment and screening work. Three to four months' time will be required from the start of recruitment to the start date of the new executive. If the executive must relocate, more time may be added. This is ample time for staff and board who are not directly involved in the search to begin transforming the agency in the direction of its future goals.

Some of the immediate work may entail addressing critical shortcomings in administrative systems. For instance, one agency was nine months overdue in completing its annual financial audit; the goal was to get it finished within three months and be on track to start preparations on the next year's audit when the new executive arrived. In another case, an agency whose programs had grown dramatically over the previous three years had woefully outdated computer systems; many of the employee records, for instance, were kept on paper. As a start to upgrading the technologies, the new fiscal year's budget was reworked to include funds to hire the agency's first technology manager. In a third agency, a deficit in middle managers' supervisory skills was identified as a major source of low staff morale; a plan for engaging a supervision trainer was drafted, with instruction to start before the new executive arrived.

Other transition goals may move the agency in the direction of the future goals that were set in the strategic review. For example, a homeless service agency that learned it needed to track its clients as they move into permanent housing in neighboring counties assigned its program director to catalog social services agencies in its tri-county placement area. When the next executive is hired, she will then choose and negotiate partnerships from among the identified agencies. The agency's board also began recruiting for new members in the county where most of the agency's clients are placed.

Similarly, a youth services agency that planned to shift programming from its own facility to school sites across the county school district began revising job descriptions and shifting staff to the school sites before the executive search was complete. In another case, an agency that trained low-income parents to get engaged in their kids' schools realized that, to gain funding for the desired expansion, it needed to document its program outcomes. During their Pivot phase, the board established a program evaluation committee to craft an impact evaluation protocol and to identify potential funders for the evaluation. The new executive, when he was hired, was tasked with reviewing protocol and acquiring the funds to do the evaluation.

As you can see, the work on upgrades and capacity-building serves two purposes. It cleans up current problems that would drag down the incoming executive. Simultaneously, it moves the agency and staff into a "new beginning" that will include a new executive director.

Tool for Letting Go of the Old and Embracing the New

Tool 11: Attending to Staff's Transition through All Three Phases

Attending to Staff Transition Needs

A second category of Pivot activities actually spans all three phases of an executive transition—interventions designed to facilitate staff movement through the human, psychological side of your leadership turnover. As William Bridges posits in his change management model, too little attention to the emotions attendant to this big change in the life of your agency can leave the participants demoralized, stuck in the past, less than fully productive, and resistant to the ways and directives of the new leader.

Tool 11 on page 64 details some ways in which the transition needs of staff can be addressed. The tool offers strategies for involving staff in consciously detaching from the departing leader, in shaping their own future as a staff group, and in engaging with the new executive. In like manner, some of the interventions may be usefully employed with board members, volunteers, and donors.

The Search

The key to a successful candidate search is to remember that it is partially a sales and promotional activity. As such, there are several components. First, the transition committee needs to determine the key selling points for the new job—the messages it will consistently spread to attract candidates. These points get crafted into a job announcement. Then, a fair application process should be devised and consideration given to how you will attract a diverse and exciting pool of applicants. Then you'll create a plan to exploit all the avenues you can to get the best applicants possible—advertising, word of mouth, networking, or whatever is most likely to uncover quality candidates for the position.

Determine and Emphasize the Job's Selling Points

To recruit a strong pool of qualified applicants, focus on the strengths of the agency and the attractions of the executive position. Recruiters—board, staff, and consultants—should be able to talk about the great services provided by the agency and the exciting challenges and opportunities facing the next executive.

The attractions can be highlighted in several ways.

Highlight your compelling mission and vision

Numerous surveys of nonprofit executives have made clear that nonprofit leaders endure in stressful jobs with below-market salaries because they want to have an impact on the quality of life in their communities. They're drawn to the mission of their agencies.

During the Prepare phase, the transition committee created an updated vision statement. That statement should communicate excitement and possibility for the future of the agency.

Attending to Staff's Transition through All Three Phases

Note: The following change management principles guide this part of the transition work:

▹ *Change* is the objective event (for example, the executive director has announced he is leaving in January of the upcoming year).

▹ *Transition* is the psychological process of reorientation triggered by the change.

▹ The *transition* process behind a change needs to be managed and attended to in order for the change to be successful.

Following are transition activities for staff:

1. Hold an all-staff meeting and meetings with small subgroups of staff.

   ▹ Present the Bridges model describing the three phases in a major transition.

   ▹ Orient staff to the human dynamics of a transition—feelings of loss, anxiety about the future, and the opportunity to create a new future.

2. Establish regular check-ins with staff throughout the transition process.

   ▹ The transition committee chair should attend the first staff meeting to explain the committee's work plan and timeline for the transition.

   ▹ Use staff meetings as a place for regular updates and to keep on top of staff concerns in the transition.

   ▹ Remind the transition and search committee to report back to staff in a timely manner on major developments.

3. Encourage the input of staff throughout the transition.

   ▹ In the scoping process—determine agency challenges and opportunities and specify what qualities are needed in the next leader through an anonymous survey and meetings with subgroups of staff.

   ▹ In the recruitment process—encourage staff to forward names of potential candidates from their networks and to help get the word out to their networks.

   ▹ In the selection process—staff representatives on the search committee will help decide which candidates should be interviewed and give all staff a chance to meet with and provide feedback on finalists.

4. Help staff to realize a good ending with the departing executive by setting up rituals such as farewell events.

5. Help staff to have a good beginning with the new executive.

   ▹ Set up a transition meeting with staff after the new executive is hired to focus on how they can support the new executive.

   ▹ Check in with staff on what's working and what concerns they have after the new executive is on the job for ninety days.

Make the job doable

CompassPoint studies on executive tenure[11] (*Daring to Lead,* 2006 and others) have documented the number one cause of executive burnout as "wearing too many hats." Executives of small and medium-sized agencies often carry responsibility for several of the many management functions—program oversight, fundraising, contracts management, personnel systems, community and public relations, information systems, and board development. If the departing executive has mentioned overload as a problem, the board should restructure the position to make the job doable.

By outlining the executive director's supervisory duties, including titles of those to be supervised, in the position announcement, candidates can see the level of administrative team support they will have.

Research has shown that, after passion for the mission, professional development

> **Tools to Aid the Search**
>
> Tool 12: Sample Job Announcement
>
> Tool 13: Sample Recruitment Plan
>
> Tool 14: Sample Memo to Board and Staff on Networking
>
> Tool 15: Summary of Typical Screening Sequence
>
> Tool 16: Sample Letter of Acknowledgment to Applicants
>
> Tool 17: Examples of First-Round Interview Questions
>
> Tool 18: Behavioral Interviewing
>
> Tool 19: Sample Candidate Rating Form
>
> Tool 20: Checking References
>
> Tool 21: Sample Agenda for Finalists' Interviews and Decision-Making Meeting
>
> Tool 22: Making a Choice
>
> Tool 23: Offer Letter Template
>
> Tool 24: Rejection Letter to Applicants Not Interviewed

ment is the second most important reason nonprofit executives take new jobs. So, the board also budgets for training and support for the next incumbent. Other considerations: Will the new executive be expected to pursue training opportunities or join a peer-learning group? Does the agency have a sabbatical leave policy? Each of these development and support benefits should be spotlighted in the announcement.

Show passion and pride in the job announcement

The dynamism of your vision and mission statements should permeate the job announcement, your main recruitment tool. Potential executive candidates want to know they would be expected to be proactive leaders of an agency proud of providing quality services in its community and eager to embrace changes that will enhance its effectiveness. They want to sense that staff and board members are excited about their contributions to the cause.

Network with excitement

Some of the most productive recruitment is in networking by phone with colleagues who could know of strong applicants who fit the candidate profile. Besides having a grasp of core information about the agency and job—programs, budget size, staff component, future directions, compensation range—networkers should be provided talking points that convey the career and community service opportunities that come with the job.

Sell the job during the interviews

Wise candidates (the kind you want) are checking out the organization while they are being screened. Candidates will wonder, *Does the interview group seem to work well together? Are they well organized and welcoming? Is there a sense of excitement in the way they talk about their agency? Are they self-assured enough to be candid about the agency challenges?*

The committee should prepare to answer questions that could be expected from the candidates. During interviews, the committee chair should field a candidate's questions and direct them to the persons who they think are best positioned to answer them.

Drafting the Job Announcement

An exciting job announcement is essential. The components include a description of the agency and its strategic goals, a description of the executive position, a list of qualifications sought in candidates, and instructions on how to apply. Tool 12 on page 67 offers a Sample Job Announcement.

The job announcement is a sales tool. Its purpose is to attract talented leaders to the position. Write it in a style that conveys enthusiasm for the mission, the work of the agency, and its future. Frame the executive position as an exciting opportunity for a passionate professional to have an important impact on the community served by the agency. The announcement should engage the reader.

Sample Job Announcement

Job Announcement

EXECUTIVE DIRECTOR

Mission Youth Services
San Francisco, California

OVERVIEW

The Board of Directors of Mission Youth Services seeks a resourceful and visionary executive leader in the field of youth services and community organizing. In partnership with board and staff, the successful candidate will be prepared to carry forward and build on the nearly thirty-year legacy of Mission Youth Services in providing academic support services and youth leadership training for young people in a diverse working-class neighborhood. He or she will create and implement strategies for significantly increasing Mission Youth Services' ability to engage local young people in creating solutions to quality-of-life problems in their community.

ABOUT MISSION YOUTH SERVICES

Established in 1979 to provide after-school tutoring and art classes for neighborhood youth, Mission Youth Services is today a highly regarded youth development agency serving the richly diverse population of the Outer Mission District in San Francisco. Its programs operate from a philosophy of "youth-in-action," which recognizes the gifts and talents of young people in the Outer Mission and works in partnership with them, their families, and the community at large to make their neighborhoods a better place in which to live and grow.

Partnership, which is at the core of Mission Youth Services' values, leads to strategies that include recruitment of board, staff, and volunteer corps members who reflect the diversity of the neighborhood and to the commitment of resources to building a multicultural, egalitarian agency culture.

Mission Youth Services programs include

- Tutoring, provided one-on-one by adult and adolescent volunteers
- Art classes
- A program of social and athletic activities tied to social services for vulnerable families and youth
- A "youth institute" that guides youth in investigating neighborhood issues and developing strategies for community change
- Neighborhood safety programs, including a collaboration between youth and merchants to form a network of safe havens on neighborhood streets

The center's annual operating budget of $1.5 million supports a full-time and part-time staff of twenty-five, plus seventy volunteers. Administrative offices are in the heart of the Outer Mission District at Mission and Delano Streets.

STRATEGIC DIRECTIONS

The Board of Directors of Mission Youth Services has adopted a set of four strategic directions designed to expand the impact of Mission Youth Services in serving the youth and improving the Outer Mission community in which they live.

▶ Expand the current two-site, after-school tutoring program into additional school-based sites.
▶ Grow the youth organizing program from its currently small corps of teenagers addressing one community issue to one with a much larger enrollment of teenagers organized to advocate for solutions to a broader array of neighborhood problems.
▶ Increase Outer Mission community representation on the board of directors; that is, move the board membership closer to representing the demographic diversity of the community.
▶ Increase program revenues from private donor sources.

BASIC FUNCTION

The executive director is directly responsible for the overall management of Mission Youth Services, including development and refinement of its service programs; control over budgeting and financial planning; contract and grant compliance; fundraising; accounting and fiscal management; and recruitment, selection, and evaluation of the management team.

REPORTING RELATIONSHIPS

The executive director reports directly to the board of directors and supervises the following:

▶ Programs director
▶ Youth institute coordinator
▶ Finance director
▶ Grants manager
▶ Administrative assistant

RESPONSIBILITIES

The executive

▶ Leads long-range planning and visioning, including assessment of community needs, in partnership with the board of directors and with staff.
▶ Oversees program development, working collaboratively with the board, programs director, and grants manager. Develops program evaluation and tracking procedures with the programs director and outside consultants.
▶ Oversees the work of the finance director in budget development and financial management in partnership with the board.
▶ Supervises development and submission of all grant proposals. Researches new funding sources. Supervises annual donor campaign, including writing some of the appeals. In collaboration with board members, meets with funders and donors.
▶ Serves as agency spokesperson responsible for public relations and acts as liaison with community agencies and businesses.
▶ Ascertains that the personnel policies of Mission Youth Services are adhered to in all hiring and employment practices. Proposes changes in policies to the board of directors. Provides for staff development activities that upgrade employee skills and motivate performance.

CANDIDATE PROFILE

Required

▷ Minimum of five years' experience in senior administrative position in a community-based nonprofit agency, including budget development and management.
▷ Significant experience working collaboratively with persons of diverse racial and ethnic backgrounds, socioeconomic statuses, ages, and sexual orientations.
▷ Minimum of three years' experience in some form of youth development work or community organizing in an inner-city neighborhood.
▷ Record of successful fundraising, from public and private sources, to support nonprofit agencies.
▷ Excellent written and oral communication skills.
▷ Bachelor's degree.

Desirable

▷ History of having led organizational growth, facilitating higher levels of mission achievement. Skills include strategic planning and management of complex internal operations and external relations.
▷ Experience in community organizing, especially with youth and young adults.
▷ Experience and familiarity with the needs and institutions of the Outer Mission District and with nonprofit funders such as city agencies and private foundations—or nonprofit work experience in a similar inner-city environment.
▷ Fluency in Spanish and/or in relevant Asian languages.

SALARY AND BENEFITS

Salary offered will be between $85,000 and $95,000, depending on the experience of the selected candidate. The benefits package includes health, dental, and disability coverage and a voluntary 403(b) retirement plan.

APPLICATION PROCESS

Applicants should send their resumes and cover letters describing their qualifications and their interest in the position to Mission Youth Services_EDsearch@WilsonAccounting.nonprofit. Deadline for applications is March 8, 2010. All applications will be kept confidential by the search committee.

Mission Youth Services is an equal opportunity employer and is committed to recruiting a broadly diverse pool of qualified candidates for this position.

Setting the Application Process

Most organizations ask candidates to submit a resume and a cover letter. The cover letter is the applicant's opportunity to tell you why she is particularly well qualified for your executive position. It also gives you a chance to see a small writing sample and to note how much attention the applicant gives to crafting a convincing letter. The candidate who sends a flat and generic cover letter may not be the enthusiastic and creative person you need to head your agency.

Some agencies will ask applicants to address a specific topic in their cover letter. A youth agency working solely with girls asked candidates to present a defense of girls-only (gender specific) youth programming, something the current executive had to do for many audiences during her tenure. The letters were measures of the applicants' abilities to craft a persuasive argument and their passions for the mission of the agency.

The job announcement should include a deadline for submitting applications—generally seven or eight weeks. Committees should be aware there are two periods in the year when recruiting is more difficult—July and August and the year-end holiday period. If possible, avoid starting a search in either of those windows.

The committee, based on earlier research, will have set the salary range for the position. Some recruiters recommend posting the chosen range in the announcement; candidates can then decide not to apply if the top of the range doesn't meet their salary expectations. Or applicants will be pulled to apply because the salary is a solid step up for them. Other recruiters suggest not listing the salary, as it may deter highly skilled candidates for whom the board would consider a higher salary. In place of naming a salary figure, these recruiters state that the salary will be commensurate with the candidate's skills and experience. Each search committee needs to decide which strategy makes most sense for its agency.

The announcement should include an e-mail address to which applications are sent. To maintain the confidentiality of the candidates' names, it's best if the e-mail box not be at the agency. Or, if it's an agency address, it should be secured in a way that only a search committee member could access it. Confidentiality is a paramount feature of search processes. Candidates have to know that no one outside of the search committee will have their names unless they become one of the three finalists. Any hint that names are not secure may potentially scare off candidates who do not want their current employer to know they are looking at another position.

Posting the Job

Your committee will need to decide how widely it wants to recruit—regionally, statewide, or nationally—and advertise accordingly. The smaller agency in a high cost-of-living city may decide to seek only local candidates if it believes the salary being offered is unlikely to pull candidates from out of town. Other agencies may require someone who already has a deep knowledge of the local culture and nonprofit sector, which means they want candidates with connections to local resources.

A large agency more likely wants to cast a wide net to pull in the best talent possible. They'll recruit aggressively and nationwide. A small agency seeking hard-to-find combinations of experience and skills will also search nationally.

A recruitment plan can help all involved in the process to follow up on their duties and contacts. Tool 13 on page 72 offers a Sample Recruitment Plan that you can adapt to your needs.

Most job advertising is done on recruiting web sites. The two sites most commonly used for nonprofit searches are OpportunityKnocks and Craigslist. Although some sites originally provided free postings for nonprofits, all sites now charge a posting fee. Creating text for an online posting will require boiling the job announcement down to a brief paragraph that conveys the essentials. The text should include a web address where the full announcement can be accessed; a preferred practice is for the searching agency to post the announcement on its own web site. The sidebar, Sample Text for Condensed Ad, on this page provides a sample paragraph derived from the position announcement example.

Sample Recruitment Plan

Job Postings

▶ Print media

  ▶ Newsletters of local, statewide, and national associations of youth development agencies

▶ Internet

  ▶ Agency web site
  ▶ CraigsList.com
  ▶ Idealist.org
  ▶ ExecSearch.coms
  ▶ Job track—alumni listing at each local university
  ▶ Other

Mailings or E-mail

▶ List of contacts generated by board members and staff

▶ Agency donors ($100+)

▶ Agency funders—foundation and government contract officers

▶ Peer agencies—list provided by county's oversight agency

Networking

▶ Follow-up calls to key persons receiving the mailing or e-mail; for instance, funders and executives of peer agencies

▶ Contacts with regional agencies or chapters based in communities of color—for example, Asian Americans/Pacific Islanders in Philanthropy (AAPIP), National Association of Black Social Workers (NABSW), Mexican American Legal Defense and Educational Fund (MALDEF)

▶ Board of directors: minimum of ten calls each to identify potential candidates

You may also choose to post the job in national or local print media. If your search is national, the *Chronicle of Philanthropy* is widely read; most agencies searching nationwide advertise in it. Others, such as the *NonProfit Times,* also list positions. Your hometown newspapers publish job openings and may be a frequently used recruiting source. You will notice that print venues charge much higher fees for postings than do online sites.

Other important resources are the web sites and newsletters of agencies that provide services similar to yours—the mayor's office of family services, the statewide association of homeless service agencies, a national network of youth development programs. Staff will know the landscape of associations and networks that connect to skilled professionals in your line of business. Some online searching may turn up more.

Networking for Candidates

Beyond the "passive" recruiting of posting the announcement and waiting for candidates to send resumes, it's critically important to actively seek qualified candidates through contacts with possible sources. When ETM services began at CompassPoint years back, one recruiter said that a good search requires two hundred phone calls. Today the number of e-mails that go out in a solid recruitment effort is many times that.

The key to successful recruiting is proactive networking via phone and e-mail. The transition committee should strongly encourage board members and staff members to use a variety of contact sources to generate candidates, including the following:

▶ Foundation professionals (especially funders for the client agency)

▶ Currently working (even happily so!) executive directors

▶ Currently working managers below the position of executive director

▶ Board members of other nonprofit agencies

▶ Colleagues that work in the corporate or private sector

Tool 14 on page 74 is a sample memo that can be used to encourage agency staff and board members to network.

Sample Memo to Board and Staff on Networking

MEMORANDUM

To: Transition Committee, Board of Directors, and Staff
From: Betsy Wilson, Chair, Mission Youth Services Executive Transition Committee
Date: January 3, 2010
Re: Active Recruitment for the Mission Youth Services Executive Director

Your transition committee has done its homework and is now beginning recruitment of Mission Youth Services' next executive director. Your participation in this outreach effort is crucial to our success.

Please take an hour (I know—we are all busy, but this is critical!) of your time in the next week to take the following steps. When you are done, *please e-mail me to let me know you've completed the task* and I will then follow up with a phone call to you.

1. First, review your own e-mail lists, Rolodexes, and address books for contacts who might be appropriate for the position of Mission Youth Services executive. Err on the side of contacting as many people as possible. So, for example, if you have a friend or colleague who works at a government agency or a corporation, keep them on your list—they just might know the perfect candidate!

2. Then, e-mail the announcement (which is in MS WORD and is attached to this e-mail message) to everyone on your list, along with a personal message along these lines:

   "I am (a board member, a staff member) of Mission Youth Services and we are looking for a new executive director. Please, just take two minutes and look at the enclosed job announcement. Ours is a great organization, and this will be a wonderful job for the right person. Please forward this message to everyone and anyone—or add it to any Listservs you might know of.

   "For more information about Mission Youth Services, please visit our web site at www.mys.nonprofit. Thanks!"

3. Please put the announcement on any Listservs that you are involved with—such as alumni groups or professional associations, *even if* they have little or no direct connection to the work of Mission Youth Services.

4. Then, think about the very best prospects that you know for our search. Not people who could DO the job, but those in the field of social services, education, or youth development who are great networkers and who are involved movers and shakers. Take the time to call these folks (leave a voice mail in the evening to save time), and let them know you forwarded (or will forward) the position announcement and that Mission Youth Services would greatly appreciate their help in getting the word out. Don't forget funders, colleagues, and other board members from other organizations.

If we can get everyone involved in active recruiting, we will have a great pool of executive candidates for Mission Youth Services. And remember, don't limit yourself to the Bay Area!

If you have any questions, or just want to brainstorm with me, please e-mail or call!

Betsy Wilson
415.555.1234
Mission Youth Services_EDSearch@WilsonAccounting.nonprofit

Each board member should be required to send the job announcement to his or her e-mail contacts. Board members should be encouraged to think of possible candidates themselves and to pursue them with an e-mail message and a follow-up phone call. A committee member might take on the duty of making sure board members fulfill their recruiting responsibilities.

If any of your board members are professionally connected to your field of service, they should be particularly active in your recruitment effort.

Staff, including the departing executive, will be rich sources of the contacts to be made in pursuit of candidates. If there is a staff person on your committee, he might coordinate staff recruitment efforts. As with the board, staff should be urged to e-mail the job announcement to all their professional and personal contacts. A basic principle in advertising is to get the message out as far and wide as possible. You never know which one will generate a buyer.

The executive director will likely have numerous contacts that could produce candidates. She should methodically move through them with e-mails and phone calls. Some of the contacts will generate a next list of contacts. The committee might offer to assist the executive in pursuing a portion of the names generated.

Another good source of candidates is the program officers in the foundations that fund your agency. Funders were good sources of information in the assessment work of the Prepare phase because of their involvement across many groups doing work similar to yours. Similarly, they are often aware of up-and-coming professionals in your field. One or two committee members should be assigned to contact them and to pursue the leads they offer.

Recruiting a Diverse Pool of Qualified Candidates

Communities are diverse, and clientele is diverse. It's essential that the leadership of community-based organizations fully represent that diversity.

The competition for talented leaders is strong. Drawing diverse talent to your top job requires focused efforts and clear messages that you are seeking candidates from the full spectrum of racial, ethnic, and cultural backgrounds.

The communications start with the position announcement. Minimally it should include the phrase "An Equal Opportunity Employer." Some CompassPoint clients have gone further with a statement such as, "We are committed to developing the leadership skills of people from diverse backgrounds.

We are committed to identifying and recruiting a broad and diverse pool of qualified candidates for this position."

When listing job qualifications, identify any cultural competencies, language proficiencies, or specific experience working with communities of color or specific social or gender identity group that are important to working with your target populations. An example might be, "Experience working with inner-city low-income high school students." Or, "Experience working with Asian American immigrant groups."

Nonprofit organizations often need executives with deep community ties or program expertise. In prioritizing qualifications, consider that an applicant who has strong community ties and programmatic experience may not have the top skills in financial management or fundraising. Consider accepting candidates with the needed community expertise and providing coaching and training for a missing administrative skill. Or, if your current director of finance is solid, the incoming executive may need less financial acumen.

In networking for candidates, there are several strategies to pursue.

▶ List the contacts your organization has across communities of color. Call the stakeholders who have connections to diverse communities that can help you to identify potential candidates and get the word out.

▶ Send the job announcement to organizations with related missions and service areas that are working with diverse constituencies.

▶ Consider conducting a national search. It provides a wider net for yielding candidates familiar with a particular minority population and its needs.

▶ Research associations of service professionals of color—for example, the National Association of Black Social Workers. Contact them about posting on a job site or Listserv for their members.

Maintaining Confidentiality for Applicants

The committee must have systems in place that provide a reasonable assurance that the identity of applicants will be kept confidential. Applicants often don't want their employers to know they are looking to move on. Some applicants fear losing face if they do not get the job. Committee ground rules should include a prohibition on members mentioning the names of applicants to anyone outside the committee.

Applications should be directed to a secure e-mail box that can be accessed only by a committee member. As a reassurance to potential candidates, it's better if their applications are sent to an e-mail address held by a committee member and not to an address inside your agency. The job announcement might also include a statement asserting that resumes will be kept confidential.

When the committee starts checking references of the two to three finalists later in the screening process, candidates know that confidentiality can no longer be maintained tightly.

Screening and Hiring

As applications arrive, the committee has to cull the better candidates from the lesser qualified. The process starts with screening resumes and concludes with board interviews of finalists. The following sections describe in detail the sequence of activities most frequently employed in CompassPoint's practice. Tool 15 on page 78 summarizes these activities.

Sorting Resumes and Choosing First-Round Candidates

One committee member should be in charge of retrieving applications from the electronic mailbox set up for the search. As resumes are received, a brief e-mail should be sent to the applicants acknowledging receipt of their materials.

Always send an acknowledgment note to applicants. Using the committee's name rather than that of a specific person can prevent unwanted calls from applicants to a committee member. Send another letter to all applicants who were not interviewed after an executive has been chosen. Interviewees usually receive a more personal note of appreciation. Tool 16 on page 79 shows a sample letter of acknowledgment.

Summary of Typical Screening Sequence

1. Two members of the committee review the full set of resumes and cover letters and sort them as follows:
   - Obviously unqualified applicants are placed in a "C list."
   - From remaining resumes, possibly qualified candidates are placed in a "B list" and probably qualified candidates in an "A list."
   - About fifteen of the top candidates are presented to the committee.

2. The entire transition committee screens resumes of the top fifteen candidates, from which they choose up to eight candidates to be invited to first-round interviews.

3. The committee interviews the first-round candidates and tentatively chooses up to three finalists.

4. The committee checks references on the tentative finalists.

5. The finalists who receive positive references are given interviews with the staff group and with the board. For candidates with questionable references, the committee decides whether to gather more information on them or to hold them back. To replace those held back, the committee may designate another first-round interviewee as a finalist and check his references.

6. Finalists have individual interviews with staff group.
   - Each finalist makes a five- to ten-minute self-presentation to the assembled staff and responds to staff questions for thirty minutes.
   - Staff provides feedback on candidates to the search committee in the form of their perceptions of the strengths and weaknesses of each in relation to the candidate profile.
   - Staff is explicitly asked not to rank the candidates. The board will consider staff input along with other information at hand when they make their choice.

7. Finalists have individual interviews with the outgoing executive. (This is often a chance for the finalists to get additional background information on the agency and the job.)

8. Board interviews the finalists, makes a tentative choice, and crafts the terms of an employment offer.

9. Optional: A background check is run on the candidate.

10. A board representative presents employment offer to the chosen candidate and negotiates the final terms, assuming no negative information comes out of a background check. A formal offer-of-employment letter is mailed to the candidate. (If a background check raises questions about the candidate's fitness for the job, the board may choose to interview the candidate again to see if the questions can be removed. Or, the board may choose to tell the candidate they have chosen not to make an offer; at that point the board would decide whether to pursue another finalist or to return to an earlier stage of the search.)

11. A start date for the new executive director is set.

12. The board issues a public statement announcing the new hire.

Begin by weeding out the obviously unqualified candidates. A common system is to give each applicant an A, B, or C. A's are those who meet all the minimum skill requirements and bring some or all of the preferred skills and experiences as well. Based on the paper screening, they show high potential. The screener definitely wants to interview these candidates. B's are the maybes. They have many of the minimum skill requirements and maybe a few of the preferred skills. Or perhaps they seem to have all the requirements and skills, but the resume gives the screener pause—a career in which no job was held for more than two years, some years unaccounted for, too little or too much detail. Or their cover letters are weak. C's are the nos, having only a few of the skills and experiences laid out in the candidate profile.

Committees handle the initial resume-sorting task in a number of ways. Some committees choose to have all members screen all resumes. Others will delegate the first screening to two or three members; the subgroup eliminates the C's and forwards all the A's and B's to the full committee. Or the committee asks the subgroup to forward only the top fifteen candidates from among the A's

TOOL 1 2 3 4 5 6 7 8 9 10 11 12 13 14 15 **16** 17 18 19 20 21 22 23 24 25 26 27 28

Sample Letter of Acknowledgment to Applicants

From: MYS_EDsearch@WilsonAccounting.nonprofit

Date: April 5, 2010

Dear Applicant Name,

This is to acknowledge our receipt of your cover letter and resume in application for the position of Executive Director at Mission Youth Services. We appreciate your interest in being a candidate for the position.

We will be in touch with you later in our search process after we have reviewed resumes and have moved into screening candidates.

Sincerely,

Transition & Search Committee
Mission Youth Services

and B's. This first sorting can wait until the reply deadline has passed or can be done as batches of resumes accumulate before the deadline.

The full committee then receives the group of resumes designated for their review. If they are looking at all the resumes, they can use the A-B-C sorting system. If the committee has only the subset of better resumes, they are asked to rank them in some more limited manner. For instance, each member could be asked to choose the top five they'd like to interview. Or they may be instructed to create their own A and B piles.

The committee then meets to discuss their individual rankings and to choose six to eight candidates to be invited to a first-round interview. There will be variances in the rankings, sometimes big ones. Place the candidates ranked in the top five or given an A by all members in a "to be interviewed" stack. Then discuss those candidates who received an A or top ranking from one or more members. When a majority decides that the committee should see a candidate, place the candidate in the "to be interviewed" stack.

A committee typically decides at the beginning of the screening process the maximum number of candidates to interview, usually six to eight. If this screening still yields too many candidates, discuss the mixed-rating candidates again, reaching consensus on which to reject. If there's uncertainty about some of the candidates, two members could have a brief phone interview with them to clear up the uncertainties. Empower the callers to decide which of the candidates should get a committee interview.

Some interviewees decline the invitation for an interview, and the committee can then raise another applicant into the list of interviewees.

At this point the committee should e-mail all of the applicants who will not be interviewed, thanking them for their interest and explaining that the committee has narrowed the pool to those best suited to the agency's needs. This important step maintains good community relations.

Sometimes a committee chooses to interview an initial two or three candidates early in the recruitment phase from among the first resumes to arrive. The advantage here is that the committee connects quickly with strong candidates from the first wave of applicants, before they are lost to competing job opportunities. A second set of candidates is then seen after the advertised closing date.

Factors to Consider in the Screening Process

▶ The candidate chosen will have a major impact on the agency's future. Investing adequate time and resources in the screening process for arriving at a good choice is important.

▶ The candidates should be screened and chosen based on the priority skills outlined in the candidate profile. It is important to keep the profile in mind at each step of the process. When there is indecision on which applicants to choose or reject, referring to the priorities can be helpful.

▶ The screening process should be done in as short a span of time as possible. The better candidates may have competing job opportunities to which they could be lost by an overly protracted process.

▶ If a particularly strong candidate comes to the fore early in the process, steps might be taken to screen him more quickly than originally planned. Certainly the person should be asked about her own job search timetable, if the committee is concerned about competing opportunities.

▶ The transition committee is responsible for all screening activities leading up to the presentation of finalists to the board for a final selection. All information on the candidates, *including their names,* must be tightly guarded by the members of the transition committee. Some desirable candidates who are currently employed elsewhere will not apply without assurance of confidentiality.

▶ Input from staff is recommended in order to provide a perspective that is distinct from the board's and to promote staff buy-in with the final choice. Staff representatives serving on the committee must be prepared to resist pressure from workmates to reveal information on candidates.

▶ The perspectives of candidates that committee members gain via interviews are important data. A second and distinct source of data is references. References called have seen the candidates in action and are a check on what the candidates say about their abilities. If questions arise about a candidate's qualifications via his references, it is sometimes appropriate to do another interview with the candidate to explore those questions. It's important to remove all significant doubts before considering offering a job.

First-Round Interviews

The goal of first-round interviews is to determine who among the semifinalists appears better qualified when screened through the lens of the candidate profile. Which candidate's style and demeanor seem like a fit with the culture of the agency? Or, if major cultural change is among the strategic directions, who seems best able to lead the change?

Scheduling the Interviews and Location

A committee member should call the candidates to schedule their interviews and explain the interview format and length. Candidates should be asked to bring a list of three references on their past work to the meeting. The committee may decide to set aside a full day for the interviews or to spread them over two days. Forty-five minutes to an hour will be needed for each interview with a fifteen-minute break between interviews.

To maintain confidentiality, the interviews should be conducted in a professional meeting space away from the agency, maybe in the offices of one of the committee members. Ideally, the space would allow for a waiting candidate

TOOL 1 2 3 4 5 6 7 8 9 10 11 12 13 14 15 16 **17** 18 19 20 21 22 23 24 25 26 27 28

Examples of First-Round Interview Questions

Crafting the questions

The search committee, with the candidate skills profile in hand, crafts a question for each skill and most of the attributes that are listed. For example, if fundraising is on the list, the committee considers what it specifically wants to ask about fundraising experience. The resulting interview questions may be one or more of the following:

▶ Tell us about your experience in creating a development plan.
▶ What was the single biggest gift you ever got on your own?
▶ What steps have you taken to expand corporate sponsorships?

This process of drafting the questions serves to bring the candidate profile back into final focus for committee members just when they need it most.

A set of sample questions

Mission

1. Please tell us why you are drawn to this position and to Mission Youth Services. What experience have you had with youth development and community organizing?

Youth development experience

2. Please describe a youth development project you were part of that you consider particularly successful in its impact on the young participants.

Community organizing experience

3. Have you had formal training in community organizing? With youth?
4. Can you describe for us a community organizing experience you've had that you consider relevant to Mission Youth Services' youth organizing work?

Experience working with diverse populations

5. Please tell us about a program or project you led that included a diverse work team. What were the essential things you did as the leader that made it a success?

to be in a room where she would not encounter an exiting interviewee. The interview room should be comfortable enough for the committee to stay in for up to a full day of interviews. Arrangements should be made for snacks and beverages. A meal would be in order if it's going to be a full day.

Selecting the Questions

Prior to seeing candidates, the committee should craft questions that will prompt the candidates to speak to how well their abilities match up with the required and preferred skills detailed in the candidate profile. A list, Examples of First-Round Interview Questions, is provided in Tool 17, pages 82 and 83. Tailor these questions to the list of abilities and experiences the organization is recruiting for.

6. What experience have you had working in communities of color? In low-income, urban communities?

Demonstrated fund development experience

7. Tell us about the strategies you have used in the past to cultivate donors for a nonprofit. What worked and what didn't? What were your biggest lessons?

Board of directors/governance

8. Describe your experience working with a board of directors. What was one lesson you've learned in working with boards about how to build a successful board and staff partnership?

Financial management

9. Tell us about your background in financial management. What is the largest budget you have managed? Give an example of a challenging financial situation you've dealt with and how you went about it.

Management style

10. How would your *supervisees* describe your management style?
11. Please describe a situation in which you had to deal with an underperforming supervisee. What worked and what didn't?

Media relations

12. Please tell us about any media or marketing campaigns that you have led or been a part of. Your role? Your success and lessons? Experience being the spokesperson?

Closing

13. Do you have any questions about what the job entails that would help you to get a better sense of whether this executive position is a good fit for you?
    Optional follow-up: What responsibility in this position do you think would stretch you the most?
14. What questions do you have for the committee?

To get comparable impressions of the interviewees, it's important they all be asked the same set of questions. Follow-up questions that probe for more details related to the scheduled questions are allowed. However, to ensure a fair and equitable process for the candidates, it's recommended that unscheduled questions not be asked. There will be a chance to roam far and wide in different formats in the next round with the finalists who emerge from this first group of interviewees.

Behavioral Questions

"Behavioral interviewing" is an important technique in screening job candidates. The committee should ask the candidate what he *has done in the past* with regard to a skill that is part of the profile, not about what he would propose to do. For example, "Please tell us about how you set up a major donor campaign in a past job and how much money was raised within the first two years" is a behavioral-style question. A weaker version would be "Please tell us how you would set up a major donor campaign for us." On page 85, Tool 18, Behavioral Interviewing, describes how to ask such questions.

Illegal Questions

There are a number of questions that cannot *by law* be asked of a candidate. In general, candidates cannot be asked about their racial, ethnic, or cultural background or about other personal matters. They can't be asked, for instance, about their marital status, about their retirement plans, about what neighborhood they live in, or if they have children. The focus must remain on skills and aptitudes for the job. As an example, you shouldn't ask, "What clubs or organizations do you belong to?" But you can ask, "What professional organizations do you belong to that you consider relevant to your ability to perform this job?" Preparing interview questions in advance and using a consistent list of questions for all candidates will reduce the chance that you will ask an off-the-cuff illegal question.

Assigning Interview Roles

Decide in advance who will ask which questions. Designate a facilitator; usually this is the committee chair. Appoint a timekeeper to signal the group when it's in danger of taking too long with any one candidate. Decide how much time to take with the candidates, usually no more than an hour each. As previously noted, ask all candidates the same set of questions in the same manner. Standardizing the first-round process ensures that all candidates are treated equally. For this reason it is recommended as well that all candidates be interviewed by the same set of people.

Behavioral Interviewing

Guidelines

▶ Look at a candidate's actual past behavior. Avoid questions that elicit speculation, such as "What would you do in XYZ situation?" Instead ask about specific examples. "Tell us about a time when XYZ happened and how you handled it."

▶ Seek specific details, including names, places, dates, and numbers.

▶ Develop questions based on job skills.

Examples

▶ Attribute: Versatility

Sample Questions:

1. "There are times when we have to adapt our behavior in order to achieve diversity. Tell us about a situation when you had to change your way of thinking in order to accommodate other points of view and about the ways in which you changed your behavior."

2. "There are often times when we have to deal with difficult people. Tell us about a time when you had to deal with a board member who was demanding and stubborn."

▶ Attribute: Creativity

Sample Questions:

1. "Describe the most creative project you ever worked on. Be specific about what you did to complete the project and how that action was creative."

2. "Give us an example of how you managed risk in order to implement a creative solution to a problem."

▶ Attribute: Leadership

Sample Questions:

1. "Please describe a work situation or an unexpected challenge in the workplace in which you demonstrated leadership. How was what you did more than just good management?"

2. "Give us an example of how you rallied support for an unpopular project or job duty among supervisees or board members. What was the outcome?"

3. "Please describe a time when you took an unpopular action in pursuit of an important goal; for example, laying off an employee in order to bring expenses in line with income. How did you prepare for doing it?"

The Interview

On the day of the interviews, the committee should convene to review the process a half hour before the first candidate arrives. When the committee is ready, the chair should escort the candidate to the interview room. The committee members greet the candidate and introduce themselves and their role with the agency. The chair makes introductory comments, outlines the interview process, and the questions begin.

The interview typically ends with the candidate asking questions of the committee that are important to her. The chair fields the questions and directs them to the appropriate committee members.

The chair closes with outlining the calendar for the screening process, indicating in general terms when the committee may be ready to make a decision on who goes to a second-round interview. If the candidate has interviewed particularly well, the chair might ask if he is considering other jobs. The strong interviewees should be encouraged to check in with the committee before deciding on a competing opportunity.

Be sure to ask for three or more references, preferably people who can speak to the candidate's skills in areas of high priority to the committee, such as starting a major donor campaign.

Documenting Impressions

Some committees use the Sample Candidate Rating Form (Tool 19 on page 88) to record significant candidate responses during the interview and to track their impressions. After each candidate leaves the room, and before any discussion, committee members record any important impressions of the candidate just interviewed and rank her in the various skill areas. Members then discuss their evaluations and perceptions of the candidate as a group. The facilitator also might ask for comments on the interview process and take recommendations for improvements. Having a written record of what candidates say and your impressions of each is important hours after you've seen numerous candidates. A more rounded discussion of candidate qualifications can result from members privately recording their thoughts before being influenced by other members' opinions.

Selecting Finalists for
Second-Round Interviews

After the last candidate has left the room, the committee should discuss the candidates with the goal of identifying two or three finalists who will be forwarded to the full board for interviews. Members might start by sharing the overall ratings they gave to each candidate. There may be quick consensus on the top one or two, with more discussion of the remaining candidates to see if there's a third who comes close. The decision should remain anchored in the question of which candidates come closest to matching the committee's profile of required skills and characteristics.

One candidate may stand head and shoulders above all the rest. In that case, the committee may consider forwarding only the one to the full board, assuming it believes it can adequately defend that position with the board.

The day following the interviews, the finalists should be called and told of their status and invited to the final set of interviews with board and staff. Tell them that their references will be called; as discussed below, they might be asked for additional references beyond ones they've volunteered. At this point also, the member making the call should inquire about the candidate's salary history. This will be important data for the board in negotiating a salary with the person chosen.

The semifinalists who did not make the cut should be called after the reference checking on the finalists has been completed, which should be about a week after their interviews. All first-round interviewees can be told at the completion of their interviews that the committee will be deciding within ten days whom to forward to the board and that they will be contacted at that point.

> **Looking Beyond Your Comfort Zone**
>
> A committee needs to check itself against giving too much weight to members' "comfort" with a particular candidate. Surveys document that minorities (in terms of race, ethnicity, class, and sexual orientation) are not in top nonprofit positions in proportion to their presence in the relevant labor pool. One reason for this is that boards unconsciously hire executives who are most like them. As one antidote to going too far on the "comfort with familiarity" dimension, a committee should set aside some of the intangibles of style and culture for a moment and scrutinize the candidates for the skills required to do the job.

Sample Candidate Rating Form

Many people find this tool useful for tracking their thoughts and the interviewee's answers during an interview. At the end of the interview, each interviewer privately gives each skill area a score. Then the committee member gives the candidate an overall score as to his fit with the profile sought in candidates. Discussions about the candidate should wait until each interviewer has made his private ratings. It's helpful if the group has a few minutes after each interview to discuss thoughts and ratings on the candidate. After all the interviews are completed, the committee has a fuller discussion and compares candidates.

In this sample, the criteria the Mission Youth Services was looking for are listed after each general category. This serves to remind the committee of the profile it is seeking in a candidate.

Mission Youth Services	**Rating:** 1 – Poor
Executive Director	2
Candidate Evaluation Form	3 – Acceptable
	4
	5 – Excellent

Candidate Name:

▶ **First Impression**: Gave compelling statement about why he/she wants this job.

Rating: _____

▶ **Youth Development Experience & Ability**: Understands youth development. Gave good examples from his/her experience. Would fit well with Mission Youth Services' programs.

Rating: _____

▶ **Community Organizing Experience**: Good grasp of organizing principles. Solid experience with youth organizing.

Rating: _____

▶ **Multicultural Experience & Leadership**: Understands what characterizes a true multicultural work environment. Provides good examples of leadership from his/her experience.

Rating: _____

▷ **Fundraising Ability**: Presents useful examples of his/her fundraising successes. Understands how to fundraise for Mission Youth Services. Would provide good leadership in FR.

Rating: _____

▷ **Financial Management**: Knows how to stay on top of the finances. Has good grasp of budgeting process.

Rating: _____

▷ **Management Style**: Seems like a good fit with staff culture at Mission Youth Services. Knows how to bring out best in staff.

Rating: _____

▷ **Board Relations**: Can challenge a board without alienating its members. Knows how to develop a board in the area of fundraising. Would communicate well with the board.

Rating: _____

▷ **Communication & Marketing Skills**: Good oral skills; understands implications of questions and makes clear and direct replies; ability to organize and present ideas. Has a good sense of how to promote Mission Youth Services with community and external stakeholders.

Rating: _____

▷ **Personal Characteristics Observed**: Personal attributes associated with a leader—credibility, integrity, judgment; ability to command respect; flexibility and adaptability; an energetic and creative self-starter who appreciates creativity.

Rating: _____

Overall Evaluation and General Fit with Mission Youth Services

Summary Rating: _____

Screening the Finalists

The decision on the three finalists should be made pending satisfactory reports from their references.

Reference Checking

Candidates' references now need to be checked. Committee members should split up the reference calls and set a short deadline for reporting the results to the chair.

Some committees may want to check references *before* the first-round interviews. However, reference checking is labor intensive and intrusive into the candidates' lives, especially in breaking the seal of confidentiality about their applications for your executive position. If asked to provide references early in the screening process, some highly qualified candidates might even withdraw their candidacies rather than have their employers know they are job hunting.

If the committee needs solid validation of a candidate's skill in a particular area, they might ask the candidate to provide additional references, specifically people who have worked with her in that area. For example, if fundraising from major donors is a critical skill, the candidate should be asked to provide the names of two people beyond the original three references who have seen her conduct a major donor campaign.

Reports from references rarely knock out a top candidate. Most often they serve to reinforce the committee's favorable opinion of a finalist. But sometimes things said will raise a question or two in a specific area. The questions raised can be posed to the candidate in an immediate phone call or in the board interviews. It's the committee's responsibility to remove as much doubt as possible about the candidate's fitness for the executive position. And a finalist deserves a chance to respond to any doubts raised.

Tool 20 on page 91 provides sample questions and guidelines when checking references.

Some agencies may also prefer to do a formal background check before finalizing a hire. In fact, some nonprofits, such as those serving children, are required to do so by law. Background checking is a second process different from reference checking. A background check, which is usually conducted for a fee by a specialized firm, covers verification of college degrees, a check for criminal history, and credit reports. Some boards choose not to do it, some will do a background check on all finalists before the board interview, and others will initiate a check only after they've decided to make a job offer.

Checking References

Guidelines

Follow the guidelines below when checking references.

▶ *Number of references*—Most committees require at least three references. The agency should request former employers, former board members that they have worked for, and even staff whom the applicant has supervised.

▶ *Disclosure to applicants*—Be sure to inform the applicant that you will be checking references. If you are planning a background check on credit status or legal matters, for instance, you will need a release signature. (More on this in the next section, Background Checks.)

▶ *What to expect*—It is important to contact current and former employers to get the best sense you can of the applicant's past experience in responsible positions at other agencies. Some employers, especially in for-profit companies, may say little, except to verify the length of employment and the title the person held. With nonprofit employers, however, there is a culture of being more forthcoming with comments on the candidate's skills and achievements.

▶ *Interpreting responses*—Listen "between the lines." If the reference is being neutral or seems to be holding back, these are key signals. Hesitation to give an applicant a good review or referral is a red flag.

▶ *Building rapport*—The conversation should start with building some rapport with the reference. Thank the person up front for the time talking with you. You might provide a brief description of your agency accompanied by your enthusiasm for its mission and work. Explain that the candidate has done well in a first interview and is now a finalist for the position. Ask about how long the interviewee has known the candidate and in what capacity.

Questions

This sequence of sample questions will help you obtain information on your candidate.

▶ Open with a broad question such as, "In what ways would you say X is a good candidate for our executive position?" Note what stands out for the interviewee and what does not get mentioned.

　▶ Follow with a succinct description of the top qualifications being sought in candidates for your position.

　▶ Follow with an open-ended question: "What can you tell me about how the candidate's skills match up with these qualifications (those not mentioned in response to the opening question)?"

▶ "Can you give me specific examples of his achievements in the area of fundraising? Or starting a new program from scratch? Or building a partnership with a new agency? Or bringing in a new donor?" The goal is to learn how well the candidate actually displayed skills in the past that you are seeking in your new executive.

▶ "Can you give me an example of how she demonstrated leadership in a particularly challenging or unexpected situation?"

▶ "What are his methods for building the abilities of supervisees?"

▶ "Please give an example of how she built teamwork among a group of staff."

▶ "In what kinds of situations does he particularly thrive?"

▶ "What situations or responsibilities are most challenging for her?"

▶ "How might we, as the board of directors for this agency, best structure our relationship with the candidate to help him have success as our executive?"

▶ "Anything else that you think we should know about the candidate?"

Background Checks

A thorough candidate screening may include a background check. Some types of agencies, such as child care centers, are required by law to conduct a background check on all employees.

Typical checks for management and professional positions include

- Social Security number check
- Criminal record check (counties of residence, seven years)
- Prior employer verification (seven years)
- Education verification (college degrees)
- Credit check (for positions of trust regarding cash, convertible inventory, or finances)

Organizations that provide fee-based background checks exist in most regions. They typically require a signed authorization and release form from the applicant. To initiate the check, the client agency submits a request form along with the candidate's signed release. For more information on the details of a background check, you can visit the web site of A Matter of Fact (www.amof.info/), a firm that conducts checks in California.

In your community, you might ask local search consultants whom they use to do background checks and the pricing.

Because a background check is so intrusive, it's recommended that it be done as a last step in the screening process and only with the candidate the board has tentatively chosen to hire. And, if your board is planning to run a background check on the finalist, the transition committee should tell each of the final three candidates. The best time to do this is after first-round interviews, when you are informing the top three interviewees that they are among the finalists. Any candidate who objects to a background check can withdraw at that point rather than after the board interview. The details on how to find a firm and the steps involved in conducting the check are provided in the sidebar Background Checks.

Involving Organization Stakeholders in Finalist Interviews

The board must interview the finalists and make a decision on whom to hire. The question for the committee is what additional information will help the board arrive at selecting the strongest candidate.

The committee may want to consider several sources of input.

- Staff—via a group interview with the full staff, the management team, or both
- Incumbent executive director—a one-on-one interview that includes giving the candidate a chance to ask questions about the nature of the job and the condition of the agency
- Board—in addition to a formal interview with the full board, a social interaction with three or four board members

STAFF INTERVIEWS

Involving staff in the interview process serves several purposes. It provides a good view on how well each candidate engages with groups—in this case, the employees they seek to lead. It gives the candidates a chance to take a measure of staff. It communicates the board's respect for staff and their importance to the agency. It makes a statement about the team culture of the agency. It also promotes staff enthusiasm for the final board choice.

The younger cohort of nonprofit professionals entering executive positions expresses a strong preference for flatter hierarchies and collaborative models of leadership. They may expect a chance to interact with staff in the screening process. Lack of staff involvement may raise questions for them about the fit between the agency culture and their leadership styles.

A staff representative from the transition committee should facilitate the staff interview. Remind staff that the final choice is the board's call. Caution staff not to rank the candidates but rather to note candidate strengths and any concerns. The facilitator should collect the comments and summarize them for the board.

To get a broader picture of the candidates' skills, ask them to make a presentation at the beginning of their sessions with staff, such as a ten-minute talk on how they would lead the agency in one of the strategic directions identified in the leadership agenda. You could ask the candidates to create a set of PowerPoint slides or to leave visual support as an option.

The board could decide only the management team will see the finalists. Again, such an interview should be managed by a committee member, include no ranking of the candidates, and be summarized for the board.

Some boards decide that candidates will not interact with staff. This is often out of a concern that staff will prefer a candidate other than the board's choice and be upset.

Protocol for Candidate Interviews with Staff

In a commonly used staff interview process

- Each finalist is scheduled for a forty-five-minute session with staff.

- One of the staff representatives from the transition committee introduces the candidate and facilitates the meeting.

- The candidate makes a brief presentation and then takes questions.

- After the candidate has left, staff members are asked about their perceptions of the strengths and shortcomings of the candidate.

- The transition committee representative prepares a succinct report on staff's impressions for use during the board's decision-making process.

The author has not seen this occur. Strong facilitation of the process will prevent most downsides. And the benefits in terms of getting an important piece of data on candidate skills and building staff morale far outweigh the slim possibility of causing problems.

INCUMBENT EXECUTIVE DIRECTOR

As with staff interviews, several important benefits are to be derived from finalist interviews with the departing executive director—assuming the nature of his departure is amicable. Such interviews provide significant data to be fed into the board selection process, promote closure with the incumbent, and expand candidates' perspectives on the job they're pursuing.

Usually, these interviews are not facilitated. The same guideline around not ranking is stressed. A committee member documents comments and perceptions from the executive after the interviews.

OTHER STAKEHOLDERS

Less commonly, the board may want the finalists to meet with other persons important to the agency's welfare. This could be an informal meeting with the founder or a session with a group of funders, volunteers, community partners, or pro bono advisors. The session could be structured similarly to the staff interview. The benefits are a broader perspective on the candidates' qualifications and buy-in from an important partner group.

BOARD SCREENING

The final events with the finalists are their interviews with the board. Prior to those formal interviews—maybe the evening before—some boards have found it useful to meet with the candidates in a less formal setting. This often takes the form of a dinner out with three or four board members. A key skill for executives is their ability to enthusiastically engage agency supporters—donors, civic leaders, funders—in a variety of ways, including over a meal. A search committee member who is already acquainted with the candidates should host the dinner.

The meals also give the candidates a chance to take their measures of the board. It's important to remember that throughout the entire screening process, the candidates are also screening the agency. Smart candidates will be impressed that the board is sufficiently committed to the agency to spend an extra evening with them.

The formal board interviews and succeeding deliberations are best scheduled to occur in one sitting. Each candidate should spend about seventy-five minutes with the board. An example of an agenda for conducting the interviews and final selection is presented in Tool 21 on this page.

TOOL 1 2 3 4 5 6 7 8 9 10 11 12 13 14 15 16 17 18 19 20 **21** 22 23 24 25 26 27 28

Sample Agenda for Finalists' Interviews and Decision-Making Meeting

MISSION YOUTH SERVICES

May 10, 2010

1. Review executive search process to date
   a. Organizational assessment summary
   b. Candidate profile: 5 priority qualifications
   c. Recruitment overview
   d. Screening history
      – 50 resumes received
      – 8 offered interviews
      – 7 interviewed
      – 2 recommended to board

2. Prepare for the interviews
   a. Present committee's profiles on the interviewees
   b. Discuss interview format
   c. Review illegal interview content, e.g., marital status

3. Interview the candidates

4. Make a choice
   a. Committee presentation on input from other sources
      – References
      – Staff
      – Outgoing executive
      – Dinner mates
   b. Board discussion and selection

5. Employment offer to chosen candidate
   a. Designation of board negotiator
   b. Offer terms (salary range and authorized upper limit; other terms)

Prior to the start of each interview, the search committee should brief the board on what they've learned about the candidates up to that point. They should suggest areas in which the board might want to focus its questioning with a particular candidate in order to augment what's known already. They should avoid stating a preference for one candidate, emphasizing that the board needs to come to its own decision. The committee should also review with the board the agency's strategic goals and the resulting candidate profile that had been put together before the search started. This helps the board focus its interviews. In assembling a list of questions for the interview, the committee might suggest some and elicit additional ones from other board members.

The search committee chair should escort each candidate into the room, have the members introduce themselves, and preview how the interview will proceed. The candidate could be asked to begin the session by making the presentation she used in her staff interview.

After all the finalists have been interviewed, the board should allot at least an hour for its deliberations. The discussion should proceed in a way that elicits the opinions of all board members on all the candidates before a decision is made. The chair might begin by asking each member to provide his impressions of candidate A, then go around the room for impressions of candidate B and then candidate C. Board members may have questions for the search committee. At this point, the chair might take a straw poll to see how board members are leaning. Once there's a clear front runner, the discussion might then center on the pros and cons of that choice. Dissenters should be asked to speak to their reluctance to go with that candidate. How does he fail to be the best choice? Could you be enthusiastic about the choice if the majority of the members stayed with it?

The goal is to reach consensus on whom to hire. This is often toughest to accomplish when choosing between two particularly good candidates. To break a deadlock, the chair might post on a flip chart the required skills delineated in the candidate profile. Board members are then asked to rate each interviewee on a scale of one to five on each skill. If the cumulative scores are particularly close, the same rating might be done with the list of preferred skills.

Once consensus is reached, the board takes a formal vote to make the choice official. If the board will be conducting a background check on the person they wish to hire (discussed in the section on reference checking, page 90), the motion to make the hire should include a clause stating the hire is pending the satisfactory outcome of a background check.

If consensus cannot be reached within a reasonable amount of time, and the board has had a full discussion of the candidate's pros and cons, it should break the deadlock with a vote. Discussions on the choice cease to be productive after about an hour. Members tend to get locked into their positions and the conversation starts getting repetitive. The chair needs to force a decision. Some additional suggestions on moving a board to reaching consensus on a choice are presented in Tool 22.

TOOL 1 2 3 4 5 6 7 8 9 10 11 12 13 14 15 16 17 18 19 20 21 **22** 23 24 25 26 27 28
Making a Choice

The board has completed its interviews with the finalists. The results of the reference checking have been reviewed, along with staff and executive director impressions. And the board remains undecided on which of two top finalists to choose.

How does the board resolve its indecision?

▷ A first strategy is to review the top five skills being sought in the next executive. Each board member privately scores the two candidates on the skills on a scale of one to five. The group's scores for each skill are compiled. Does one of the two candidates score significantly higher than the other? Where there is wide divergence in scoring a candidate on a particular skill, for instance, ones and fives, discuss the opposing viewpoints. Chart the pros and cons for each candidate on each skill. Use a flip chart as a visual aid to elucidating significant differences among the candidates. Are board members moved to change their choice?

▷ If there are still uncertainties about the candidates' abilities in some areas, the board might invite the two candidates back for another interview. The focus could be on comparing their abilities in the top five skill areas identified in the candidate profile. The interviews might be at a different time of day than the previous interviews to test the candidates' acuity in a different situation. Or the candidates could be asked to prepare a ten-minute presentation on a topic different from the one covered in the first interview with the board.

▷ Ideally, the board would like to have consensus on its choice. If the board is close to consensus—there are just two or three opposing board members—the holdouts can be asked if they will "step aside." This means that their objections to the candidate of the majority are not serious enough for them to block consensus. If the choice is between two strong candidates, this option typically results in full consensus.

▷ If consensus cannot be reached, the chair may declare that the choice will be made by a majority vote. If before voting the board has first had a full discussion in which the minority opinions have been fully aired, those in the minority will likely accept the choice and move forward supporting the chosen executive.

Making a Hire

The board chair should call to inform and congratulate the choice and to convey the board's enthusiasm for having her as the agency's chief executive. If a background check is to be conducted, the chair should arrange that with the candidate.

The chair should negotiate the terms of employment, including a start date. He should offer a salary at the lower end of the authorized range and not move above the top end without going back to the board. If the candidate is from out of town, the chair should discuss relocation funds. If the board will be doing a background check, the chair should be clear with the candidate that the employment offer stands, pending a satisfactory outcome with the background check.

The candidate may push for benefits beyond the standard package given to employees, such as an additional week of vacation. However, special benefits are best avoided unless the board believes they should be agreed to for an exceptional candidate as an alternative to raising the salary beyond the board's comfort level.

Boards are correctly wary of executives who demand special treatment or compensation or benefits beyond industry norms. If the board has done its homework in ensuring its employee package is similar to those of peer agencies, requests to add things on for an executive generally should be rejected. Acceding to extraordinary requests now can mean being faced with even bigger ones later. An executive out of tune with his board and staff is rarely successful in the job for long.

Once the background check has been completed and the terms of employment agreed to, the chair mails an employment offer letter to the chosen executive. An Offer Letter Template is provided in Tool 23 on page 99. Ask the candidate to approve the terms by adding his signature to the letter and returning it.

Offer Letter Template

AGENCY LETTERHEAD

May 5, 2010

Anna Lopez
360 63rd St
San Francisco, CA 94123

Dear Anna:

The Board of Directors of Mission Youth Services is pleased to extend to you an offer of employment as executive director. The following outlines the specific details of the offer.

1. A base salary of $ _____ per year, reviewable annually on the anniversary of hire.

2. An executive benefits package consistent with Mission Youth Services' existing policies and consisting of the following:

Vacation:	Life insurance:
Holidays:	Disability insurance:
Sick leave:	Retirement savings plan:
Health & dental coverage:	

3. The Board of Directors will meet with you a month after the start of your tenure to set performance goals and the protocol for evaluating your performance. The board will evaluate your performance after your first six months of employment.

4. Although Mission Youth Services expects that the relationship with you will be long term and mutually rewarding, both you and Mission Youth Services have the right to terminate employment at any time for any reason.

5. Employment as executive director is to begin on June 1, 2010.

On behalf of the Board of Directors of Mission Youth Services, I am delighted to extend the offer and look forward to a long and close professional relationship.

I ask that you confirm your acceptance of this offer by signing below. Please keep a copy for your files and return the original to me in the enclosed envelope.

Sincerely,

Betsy Wilson
Board Chair
Mission Youth Services

I, _____, accept the terms of this offer.

_____   _____
Signature   Date

At this point, the chair should call the other two finalists, tell them the decision, and thank them. They should not be given any details as to why they were not the board's choice other than the fact that the board carefully deliberated the qualifications of the three finalists and decided the one chosen is the best fit for the agency's needs—"You were great; it was a tough choice; thank you."

For the rest of the applicants, a formal note of thanks from the board chair serves to cement their regard for your agency. For the candidates interviewed in the first round, a letter sent via the U.S. Postal Service communicates solid appreciation. If a message was not sent earlier to the rest of the applicants, an e-mail statement from the board chair at this point would be in order. A sample letter for those applicants not interviewed is provided in Tool 24.

TOOL 1 2 3 4 5 6 7 8 9 10 11 12 13 14 15 16 17 18 19 20 21 22 23 **24** 25 26 27 28

Rejection Letter to Applicants Not Interviewed

AGENCY LETTERHEAD

Date

Mission Youth Services Applicant
Address
City, State & Zip code

Dear Applicant:

This is to inform you that we have hired Anna Lopez as the new executive director of Mission Youth Services.

I very much appreciate your interest in the position and the attention you gave to applying. We received a large number of resumes and faced the tough task of choosing from among many qualified applicants.

Best wishes in all your professional pursuits.

Gratefully,

Betsy Wilson
Chair
Board of Directors

▲ ▲ ▲

Phew! You've made it through perhaps the most nerve-racking part of the process—identifying your organization's next leader. Indeed, the Pivot phase of executive transition is extremely busy. Your organization has upgraded its capacity. It has conducted an extensive search, recruiting top candidates from a diverse field—and finally choosing the new director. Now you're ready to set the foundation for this individual's transition into leadership. Chapter Five will address each of the areas we recommend you pay attention to.

Chapter Five:
Thrive

5

▶ Thrive, the third phase of executive transition, is important to maximizing the new executive's chances of successfully pursuing the agency's strategic directions. Chapter Five presents processes an agency can use to ease a new executive into his job and to establish smooth organizational relationships—in other words, how to best set a strong foundation from which a new executive and the agency can move forward and thrive. Topics covered include creating an orientation plan, setting appropriate performance goals and evaluation procedures for the new executive, building the board and executive team, and the importance of ongoing professional development for the executive.

Getting Started

The transition and search committee, having given months of their time, first to arriving at the leadership agenda for the agency and then to recruiting and screening candidates, is likely exhausted. They want to be hailed for a job well done and to retire. But for the agency to arrive at the full fruits of its labors, it's important that the committee arrange for the final round of activities that serve to set the new leader with what he needs to succeed.

Some transition and search committees will hand off responsibility for the Thrive phase to a new group of two or three board members who bring fresh energy. However, it's helpful to the continuity of the work if one of the Thrive committee members is a veteran of the transition committee. The Thrive committee will report to the executive committee on its work with the executive and on agreements made with her.

> **Tools for Orientation**
>
> Tool 25: Hiring Announcement Letter
>
> Tool 26: Sample New Executive Director Orientation Plan

Orientation

A first step is to introduce the new executive director to the agency's constituencies—staff being chief among them. For staff, one potent ritual is for the board chair to convene a full staff meeting on the morning of the new executive's first day, at which the chair presents the new staff leader. Other board members may attend as well.

The chair reviews in brief the full transition process that ended in the board's hire of the new executive. Staff who served on the committee are thanked, and all staff are thanked for their input at various points along the way. The departing executive is acknowledged for her achievements. And finally the chair offers some details about how the new executive is the right person to lead staff in its pursuit of the agency's strategic directions. Staff can extend a welcome and a brief reception may follow.

For external constituencies, send a letter over the board chair's signature to all the agency's stakeholders announcing the hire and expressing excitement for the future work of the agency. See Tool 25 on page 105 for a sample hiring announcement.

It's important to begin scheduling meetings for the new executive with the major supporters of the agency. For meetings with supporters who were especially close to the previous executive, he might accompany the new executive.

These introductions are one piece of a more expansive orientation plan that should be mapped out before the new executive starts work. An example of a fulsome orientation plan is in Tool 26 on page 106.

Hiring Announcement Letter

AGENCY LETTERHEAD

Date

Friend of Mission Youth Services
Address
City, State & Zip code

Dear Friend:

On behalf of the Board of Directors of Mission Youth Services, I am pleased to announce that Anna Lopez has accepted the position of executive director of Mission Youth Services. In trying to fill the shoes of Lincoln Chiu, Mission Youth Services' Board of Directors faced the daunting challenge of identifying Mission Youth Services' unique strengths and challenges, articulating a powerful vision for the future of our youth development work, and finding the right leader for that future.

As anyone who has had the opportunity to work with Anna knows, she has extensive expertise in the fields of youth development and community organizing. We are especially fortunate that Anna brings hands-on experience in developing and managing programs and services so similar to those of Mission Youth Services from her five-year tenure as associate director at the Encino Boys and Girls Club in Southern California. Anna got her start in youth work as a counselor in a truancy prevention program in Encino, where she participated in the creation of a highly successful alternative education track in the local school system.

Anna will begin her role as executive director on June 1, and I know she is looking forward to working with you. I want to thank you for your ongoing support of Mission Youth Services, especially during this time of leadership transition. I can assure you that the board of directors, together with staff, is committed to continuing Mission Youth Services' splendid record of success.

Sincerely,

Betsy Wilson
Chair
Board of Directors

Sample New Executive Director Orientation Plan

A formal orientation ensures a good beginning for the new executive. The list of activities below offers a model of what might be included in the orientation. The board should conduct the activities, if possible.

▶ *Before starting work, send the new chief executive a letter of welcome to the organization.* Verify the starting date and provide a copy of the employee policies and procedures manual. (This can be included in the offer letter.)

▶ *At this point, the board may send a letter to stakeholders.* The letter should announce the new executive by name, state when he is starting, tell something about the executive's background, and ask stakeholders to call the board chair if they have any questions or concerns.

▶ *Brief the new chief executive on important information.* Review the organization chart, last year's final report, the strategic plan, this year's budget, and the employee policies and procedure manual. In the same meeting, explain the performance review procedure and provide him a copy of the performance review document.

▶ *Hold an introductory meeting with staff.* When the new chief executive begins employment (or before if possible), introduce him to staff in a meeting dedicated to this purpose. If the organization is small enough, have all staff attend and introduce themselves. If the organization is larger, invite all managers to the meeting and have the managers introduce themselves.

▶ *Ensure the new chief executive receives necessary materials and is familiar with the facilities.* Ensure an assistant gives her keys and has her sign tax and benefit forms. Review the layout of offices, bathrooms, storage areas, kitchen use, copy and fax systems, computer configuration and procedures, telephone usage, and any special billing procedures for use of office systems.

▶ *Schedule any needed training.* For example, map out computer training, including use of passwords, overview of software and documentation, location and use of peripherals, and where to go to get questions answered.

▶ *Review policies and procedures about use of facilities.*

▶ *Assign a board member to be the new chief executive's "buddy."* This person should remain available to answer any questions over the next four weeks.

▶ *Treat the new chief executive to lunch.* Have someone take him to lunch on the first day of work and invite other staff members along.

▶ *During the first six weeks, arrange one-on-one meetings between board members and the new chief executive.* The goal is to establish good working relationships between the executive and board members. The executive can learn of the members' particular interests regarding the programs of the agency and of what they offer in terms of skills and resources. Board members can extend offers of support for helping the executive get grounded in the work of the agency.

The outgoing leader is, of course, a major source of information for the new executive. When possible she should be on site for the first few days of the new leader's tenure. A week is plenty. The new executive will hit his absorption limit within that time and will be eager to make the job fully his. For the next few weeks the previous executive can be a great help by being available to answer questions as they arise.

Performance Goals and Evaluation

The new executive needs clear performance priorities and feedback on how he is doing, especially during the first months with the organization. The Thrive committee will present to the new executive the measurable performance priorities that were created as the last piece of the leadership agenda (Tool 8, page 55) in the Prepare phase. These objectives are the committee's best estimate of what needs to be done and can be achieved by the new leader. However, after the executive has been on the job for a few weeks, he will develop a good sense of what's possible with the resources at hand. It's important to schedule a meeting with him about six weeks after his entry to get his newly informed perspective on how realistic the objectives are. In the sample priorities set by the Mission Youth Services committee, for instance, the recently installed director may have discovered that the donor database is in serious disarray. He asks that the first-year goal be reduced to a 25 percent increase in private donors while he works to improve fundraising operations.

Further, the organization should prepare for the executive's annual evaluation, by which the board will evaluate the executive on his progress toward the agency's goals and in other leadership and management arenas.

Performance Goals

In composing the leadership agenda in the Prepare phase, the transition committee translated the agency's strategic directions and capacity-building needs into performance priorities to be shared with the executive to be hired. A couple of weeks after the new executive starts, the Thrive committee meets with the executive to discuss the leadership agenda and the related performance goals. The meeting will also include additional pieces of the Thrive phase described below.

Tools to Aid Performance Goals and Evaluation

Tool 27: Sample Set of Executive Performance Goals

Tool 28: Executive Director Annual Assessment Form

The committee and executive should also review any capacity upgrades that the organization pursued during the Pivot phase. Overseeing the ongoing work on those objectives becomes the responsibility of the executive.

The leadership agenda and performance goals tell the executive where to focus and what the board expects of her.

Revisit the performance goals with the executive after his first two months on the job. Once familiar with both staff and the resources, the executive will have a better sense of what's realistically achievable. For instance, having spoken with the city's coordinator of homeless services and other probable funding sources, the executive may realize it will take eighteen months to get the proposed transitional housing program in place. The board's twelve-month benchmark goal could be revised to say that the executive will have secured 80 percent of the funding needed by then.

Performance Evaluation System

Because the executive director is so central to the success or failure of the agency, evaluation of the executive director by the board is an important component of the board's responsibilities. An annual, written evaluation documents

TOOL 1 2 3 4 5 6 7 8 9 10 11 12 13 14 15 16 17 18 19 20 21 22 23 24 25 26 **27** 28

Sample Set of Executive Performance Goals

First-year performance priorities for the new executive

▸ Open a Mission Youth Services after-school tutoring program in two additional public schools.

▸ Convert the "youth organizing program" into a "youth empowerment department" at Mission Youth Services that has at least twenty-five youth enrolled who are beginning to address two local community needs.

▸ Acquire grants from at least two new foundations to support the youth empowerment department.

▸ Increase the number of private individual donors to Mission Youth Services by 50 percent.

▸ Raise the visibility of Mission Youth Services' programs with the government officials representing the neighborhoods of Mission Youth Services.

the executive director's achievements, identifies performance areas needing improvement, and helps the executive director understand where the board is insufficiently informed. Typically, a committee of the board (often the board officers) leads the evaluation process, reports on the evaluation to the entire board, and recommends salary for the next year.

Because the executive director acts both directly and indirectly through others to manage the organization, evaluating the executive director's performance is inevitably linked to evaluating the agency's performance as a whole. As a result, many boards incorporate evaluation of the executive director into the annual review of organizational performance and goal-setting for the coming year.

Most boards of directors involve only other board members directly in the evaluation process. Others choose to add feedback from staff on the executive director's work. Still others go outside the agency to gather information regarding the performance of both the agency and the executive director; for example, to funders, collaborating agencies, volunteers, and clients.

Regardless of the evaluation process used, executive directors need feedback year-round. Like any employee, executive directors need praise and acknowledgment for work well done and immediate feedback when problems arise. In the best situations, the board president and officers have established good working relationships with the executive director where constant feedback flows in both directions. The annual formal evaluation is an important component of, not a substitute for, that relationship.

The first part of the annual evaluation covers the executive's achievements on his twelve-month performance goals. Those goals were based on the agency's strategic directions for the year. Goals achieved should be fully acknowledged. Where goals were not reached, the reasons why should be examined. A fresh set of goals that move the agency in the direction of its strategic goals is then set for the next twelve months.

The second part of the evaluation can look something like Tool 28, the Executive Director Annual Assessment Form (on page 110). It provides a format for evaluating your executive on generic management and leadership duties. It is best used as a draft from which you can create your own tool. You might, for instance, add questions related to legislative advocacy or meeting with the press. You should adapt these questions to fit your organization's work.

Executive Director Annual Assessment Form

Please rate your assessment of each category of performance as Remarkable (R), Satisfactory (S), Unsatisfactory (U), or Unknown (Unk)

Organization Wide: Program Development and Delivery *(Circle one)*

1. Ensures that the organization has a long-range strategy that achieves its mission and toward which it makes consistent and timely progress.

    R S U Unk

2. Provides effective leadership in developing program and organizational plans with the board of directors and staff.

    R S U Unk

3. Meets or exceeds program goals in quantity and quality.

    R S U Unk

4. Evaluates how well goals and objectives have been met.

    R S U Unk

5. Demonstrates quality of analysis and judgment in program planning, implementation, and evaluation.

    R S U Unk

6. Shows creativity and initiative in creating new programs.

    R S U Unk

7. Maintains and utilizes a working knowledge of significant developments and trends in the field (such as AIDS, developmental disabilities, community theater, or sustainable agriculture) and in the relevant community (such as neighborhood, city, Latino engineers, or health seniors).

    R S U Unk

Comments:

Administration and Human Resource Management

1. Organizes and assigns work effectively, delegating appropriate levels of freedom and authority.

    R S U Unk

2. Establishes and makes use of an effective management team.

    R S U Unk

3. Maintains appropriate balance between administration and programs.

    R S U Unk

4. Ensures that job descriptions are developed and that regular performance evaluations are held and documented.

> R S U Unk

5. Ensures compliance with personnel policies and state and federal regulations on workplaces and employment.

> R S U Unk

6. Ensures that employees are licensed and credentialed as required and that appropriate background checks are conducted.

> R S U Unk

7. Ensures that dimensions of diversity (race, gender, age, sexual orientation, economic background, etc.) are identified as important to the organization's mission and business goals and recruits and retains a diverse staff.

> R S U Unk

8. Ensures that policies and procedures are in place to maximize volunteer involvement.

> R S U Unk

9. Encourages staff development and education and assists program staff in relating their specialized work to the total program of the organization. Leadership development is embedded in organizational practices as appropriate.

> R S U Unk

10. Maintains a climate that attracts, keeps, and motivates a diverse staff of top-quality people.

> R S U Unk

Comments:

Community Relations

1. Serves as an effective spokesperson for the organization; represents the programs and point of view of the organization to other nonprofits, government, foundations, corporations, and the general public.

> R S U Unk

2. Establishes sound working relationships and cooperative arrangements with community groups and organizations.

> R S U Unk

Comments:

Financial Management and Legal Compliance

1. Assures adequate control and accounting of all funds, including developing and maintaining sound financial practices.

   R S U Unk

2. Works with staff, finance committee, and the board in preparing a budget; sees that the organization operates within budget guidelines.

   R S U Unk

3. Maintains official records and documents, and ensures compliance with federal, state, and local regulations and reporting requirements (such as annual information returns; payroll withholding and reporting).

   R S U Unk

4. Executes legal documents appropriately.

   R S U Unk

5. Assures that funds are disbursed in accordance with contract requirements and donor designations.

   R S U Unk

Comments:

Fundraising

1. Develops realistic, ambitious fundraising plans.

   R S U Unk

2. Meets or exceeds revenue goals, ensuring that adequate funds are available to permit the organization to carry out its work.

   R S U Unk

3. Successfully involves others in fundraising.

   R S U Unk

4. Establishes positive relationships with government, foundation, and corporate funders.

   R S U Unk

5. Establishes positive relationships with individual donors.

   R S U Unk

Comments:

Board of Directors

1. Works well with board officers.

    R S U Unk

2. Provides appropriate, adequate, and timely information to the board.

    R S U Unk

3. Provides support to board committees.

    R S U Unk

4. Sees that the board is kept informed on the condition of the organization and all important factors influencing it.

    R S U Unk

5. Works effectively with the board as a whole. Appropriately balances supporting the board and providing leadership to the board.

    R S U Unk

Comments:

Are there specific performance objectives, either for the executive director or for the agency as a whole, which you would suggest we add for the coming year?

Are there any other comments you would like to make?

+ +
This evaluation form was developed by Jan Masaoka, former Executive Director of CompassPoint, and first published in CompassPoint's online newsletter, *Board Café,* in 1999. Reprinted with permission.
+ +

Building the Board and Executive Team

The relationship between the board and new executive needs careful attention. Communications should be such that any problems that arise can be addressed quickly, candidly, and respectfully. Three actions that will help in building the board and executive team are to craft a mutually supportive partnership, establish solid communication patterns, and state board expectations for executive support.

Craft a Mutually Supportive Partnership

An executive's job is an inherently tough one. In small to medium-sized nonprofits, the span of direct executive responsibilities, from financial oversight to program development to community collaborations, is enormous. Too much to do, along with feelings of isolation at the top of staff hierarchy, are the main causes of executive burnout. A solid partnership between the board and the executive can mitigate those problems and heighten agency achievements.

The board and executive can help their relationship by clearly stating their mutual expectations. A supportive board will periodically ask the executive director if the board might be more helpful in some way. For instance, a board member can research new vendors for staff health insurance plans when the agency is seeking to cut healthcare costs. Or, the board can offer to set up a board committee to produce the summer staff picnic that's been a big morale booster but a drain on administrative energies. Even a small investment in supporting their executive can save the board the much greater time and energy demanded in searching for a new executive.

Conversely, the executive has an obligation to support the board of directors. Board members are volunteers, usually with limited time to give to board duties. The executive works with them to make sure their talents are efficiently tapped. When a board needs consulting or training, the executive will often recruit the resources. Successful executives report that board development is high on their list of priorities.

Establish Solid Communication Patterns

It is important to both parties that the executive establish solid communication links with the board, especially the executive committee members. For the new executive, the executive committee might set up two or three special meetings with him in the first two months of the new tenure to respond to issues and questions that arise.

Typically, the executive and the board president communicate frequently by phone and e-mail. They might establish a specific time each week during the first few months of the new tenure for a phone check-in. If the board president is particularly pressed by her own job demands, another executive committee member might be designated as the "buddy" for the executive.

Common questions to consider in setting up communication patterns between the executive director and board president are

▶ Does the board chair prefer phone calls or e-mail? (Note: E-mail can facilitate quick communications. However, care should be taken not to put in print anything that cannot be publicly shared.)

▶ How often does the board chair expect to hear from the executive?

▶ What topics would the executive like to discuss with the chair?

▶ Can chair and executive agree that they will respond to one another's messages within twenty-four hours?

State Board Expectations for Executive Support

Each agency has a different protocol for what staff support the board receives. The board can ensure its expectations will be met by making the protocol explicit. Having these straightforward discussions at the start of the new relationship sets a pattern that will be helpful to resolving any problems that arise down the road. All parties will have developed the habit of speaking directly to their needs and negotiating differences in expectations.

Common questions to consider in setting up board communications protocols are

▶ How does the agenda get set for the monthly board meeting?

▶ What does the executive contribute to the meeting?

▶ Who handles the logistics for board meetings—room reservation, food, packet mailings, and so forth?

▶ Who decides what's in the board packet?

▶ Who attends the board committee meetings?

▶ What clerical support has been provided to the board?

Professional Development for the New Executive

Another important step in ensuring a good beginning for the new executive is the creation of a professional development and support plan. Studies of nonprofit employees find that they join your agency primarily out of commitment to your mission. And they will stay with your agency if they see a significant impact from their work, their salaries remain competitive, and they have opportunities for professional development.

A development plan for an executive director should give priority to the skills most critical to leading your agency. The person you hired is high on passion for your cause and is skilled in many areas but likely falls short of having all the components listed in your candidate profile. That's where professional development can help. Surveys have documented that close to two-thirds of new executives are in the top job for the first time.[12] Yet even veterans can benefit from professional development geared to helping them master the complexities of the job. The better executive will be continually looking to improve leadership and management abilities and will not see pursuit of training or coaching as a sign of weakness.

The Thrive committee should explore with the executive what forms of professional training and support would be helpful. Initially, the discussion could focus on the strategic directions the executive is expected to pursue. What new skills does the executive need to reach the strategic goals?

Support and skill-building come from many sources. A coach or mentor can be particularly effective in helping an executive to identify how to build on existing talents and to arrange the job to maximize fit. Classes are available from a number of sources. The local university may offer courses leading to certification in a specific area such as fundraising or human resources management. A peer support group might help the executive to understand the local nonprofit landscape and common executive dilemmas. Successful, longer tenured executives report having connected early in their jobs with an empathetic professional peer or peers with whom they could air their triumphs and tribulations.

The following menu of training and support offers suggestions for what might be written into the professional development plan of your entering executive.

TRAINING

▷ College courses leading to a degree or a specialty certificate, such as fundraising

▷ Workshops from a nonprofit support center or a commercial training enterprise

▷ Consultation to train the executive in a needed area, such as team building with staff

▷ Online resources, which allow for self-paced learning

▷ Conferences, which feature both technical skill development and networking

COACHING AND MENTORING

▷ Executive coaching, to help and support the new leader's development

▷ Mentoring, provided by a current or former executive with experience running a similar agency

PEER NETWORKING

▷ Informal connections with executives facing similar challenges

▷ Formal peer groups, which meet regularly and have an agenda and learning goals

▷ Industry associations, which are membership groups of similar agencies that provide networking and learning opportunities at conferences and regional meetings

The executive should identify professional development goals for the year for the committee. Ideally the agency budget has a line item covering staff development. If not, the committee will work with the executive to budget money to support the executive's plan. At the twelve-month evaluation point, progress on the executive's development goals is reviewed.

▲ ▲ ▲

At the end of three or four months, the Thrive committee should have a final meeting with the executive to check on her progress at having settled into the job. Assuming things are going well, the committee then dissolves and submits a brief written report to the executive committee detailing work done and agreements made with the executive, such as the list of performance goals. The executive's primary source of feedback and support then becomes the executive committee.

If the committee feels the new executive is not solidly grounded at the end of three or four months, or believes there are problems with his performance, it's best to identify the problems as concretely and quickly as possible and devise solutions. Unaddressed problems of underperformance in the early stages of his tenure could well fester until they become big problems for the agency and its programs. The committee might first consider whether they expected too much achievement too soon. Are you holding him to too high a standard too soon? If it's not a matter of unrealistic expectations, the committee might look to identify what additional support or training the executive needs, such as a coach to help him develop his fit with his job. A short-term performance improvement plan might be crafted with the committee staying in place to monitor its implementation and outcomes.

With the conclusion of the Thrive phase (and this chapter), you've now learned the major executive transition steps an organization needs to address in the process of selecting a new leader: preparation and development of a recruitment and selection plan, implementation of your plan, and easing your new executive into the organization and onto the job. But you're not done yet. Chapter Six discusses some of the key transition-related considerations that may need to be factored into your organization's transition process.

Chapter Six:
Transition Topics

▶ So far, we've focused on the ideal steps in helping an organization Prepare, Pivot, and Thrive through an executive transition. In this chapter we'll explore some common transition topics that we encounter with clients. Some, but probably not all, may be relevant to the needs of your agency's particular transition. You can skip topics that don't apply to your situation, but it still may be useful to skim them; you might catch an issue that your agency needs to consider but hasn't. For agencies facing a gap between executives, there's a discussion of interim executive directors—the skills needed, what to expect of interim executives, and how to screen them. And if your board is looking to hire a recruiting firm, there's advice on how to pick one that will be a good fit for your organization.

Considerations for the Long-Tenured Executive

The ETM model provides a set of basic steps that facilitate a successful and productive transition. The work typically takes from four to six months to complete. A board takes the first step when it learns its executive director will be leaving her position shortly.

In our decade of assisting agencies with their leadership transitions, we've found that the six-month ETM model is inadequate for dealing with the departures of long-term executives, especially those who founded their agencies. Executives who have been on the job for ten years or

Special Transition Topics

This chapter covers special topics that apply to some, but not every, executive transition. These topics include:

Considerations for the
Long-Tenured Executive . . . . page 119

The Role of the Departing Executive . . page 123

Dealing with Internal Candidates . . . . page 125

Crafting Exit Packages . . . . page 126

Grooming a Successor . . . . page 127

Embracing Diversity and Difference . . page 128

Using an Interim Executive . . . . page 129

Choosing and Using Consultants
and Recruiters . . . . page 131

more, and who have been successful in growing reputable and highly valued community services, have often merged their identities with those of their agencies. They are dominant figures within their agencies and in the community. They've designed the programs and administrative systems in ways that fit their talents and visions. Board and staff follow their lead in the major decisions facing their agencies. Funders and other community members assume the ongoing success of their agencies is highly dependent on their presence.

When the "long and strong" executive pulls out with no more than a couple months' preparation, the agency too often goes into a period of serious decline. An early transition client of CompassPoint, in which the executive of thirty-two years left with three months' notice, immediately fell into difficult straits. The top financial officer left almost simultaneously with the executive. The high-wire act he and the executive had developed to keep the $7.5 million agency solvent in tough financial times could not be duplicated by others. The chief of operations and property management was relatively new and unable to function once the close support of the executive was gone. The near bankruptcy that quickly developed caused the board to bring in an interim executive. She had to sell off some programs and some properties. Twelve months later the agency stabilized at a budget level of $3 million. There are stories of other valued agencies closing down entirely after their quarter-century executives left.

Whether via emergency or a planned departure, your organization must prepare for the eventual departure of its executive. Called *succession planning,* this can be a delicate topic for a board to raise with its executive. You need to take pains to reassure him that you are not suggesting he consider leaving—that you are not pushing him toward the door.

The topic of succession planning is beyond the scope of this book. However, we will touch on a few of the areas that board, executive, and staff should be working on—even when the executive is not (yet) a long-tenured one: *departure-defined succession planning, strategic leader development,* and *emergency succession planning.*

Departure-Defined Succession Planning

CompassPoint, working closely with TransitionGuides,[13] has developed a succession-planning protocol for working with long-term executives and their boards prior to scheduled exits. Labeled "departure-defined succession planning," the work gives significant attention over eighteen months or more to building the capacity of the board, managers, and systems to sustain funding and programs beyond the current executive's tenure.[14]

This succession-planning process most frequently starts with assistance to the executive in her private deliberations about when to leave and in addressing the issues, personal and professional, that would inhibit her from letting go. The work then moves to increasing the leadership strength of board and managers so as to reduce their dependency upon the skills, charisma, and relationships of the incumbent executive and to "stand strong" without her presence.

As the executive begins to develop an awareness that it's time to leave—because he sees the agency needs fresh leadership to take it forward—he has to resolve personal issues (I still need a good salary to survive financially) and professional issues (I'm reluctant to give up this position of community influence) before he can make a firm decision. Outside assistance, such as a career coach, can be helpful. Until the executive's barriers to letting go are resolved and a departure date is set, the next phase of succession planning cannot take off.

Basically, this next period of succession planning takes the Prepare phase of the ETM model and expands on it dramatically in scope and duration—up to eighteen months. A "sustainability audit" is recommended that looks at what vulnerabilities might come to the fore in management systems, in staff capabilities, with the board, and in finances when the executive departs. Plans are then made for mitigating the vulnerabilities. For example, the entrepreneurial executive often uniquely holds the majority of the relationships with foundation funders and major donors. Those important supporters need to solidly connect with someone else in the agency *before* the executive leaves. The long-tenured leader often has accrued a span of responsibilities too impossibly broad for a single successor, no matter how skilled, to take on. An administrative restructure is in order to make the top job doable. The management team may not be a true leadership team in that the executive makes all major decisions and consults only sporadically with his deputies; managers compete with one another for resources and have no history of group decision making. The agency may need to engage a coach to help build a culture of shared leadership to reduce dependence on the single executive decision-maker. Similarly, the board may not have developed its governance muscles; it has traditionally taken directions from the executive and not asked many questions.

While the executive is shoring up systems and looking to solidify the management and leadership abilities of staff, she also should be negotiating with the board the boundaries on whatever role she will have with the agency after the next executive is hired. The section below on the role of the departing executive provides guidelines for this important succession-planning element. Board failure to address this piece can result in a frustrated successor who leaves because of having to share power with a predecessor who never really gave up control. The emeritus leader needs to move out of the office, both literally and figuratively, and be on call to support the ways and the work of the new leader.

And finally, as with the executive transitions model, the agency needs to spend time updating its vision and strategic directions. The succession-planning process concludes with the recruitment and hiring of a new executive with the skills and experience to successfully pursue those directions.

Strategic Leader Development

We recommend that agencies consider another form of succession planning regardless of whether an executive departure is on the horizon. Titled *strategic leader development,* this approach to succession entails ongoing professional development centered on first defining an agency's strategic vision, on identifying the leadership and managerial skills necessary to carry out that vision, and on recruiting and maintaining a staff of talented individuals who have (or can develop) those skills. In our training course at CompassPoint for new nonprofit leaders, we recommend that executives start this type of succession planning as soon as they start their jobs.

An organization that gives ongoing attention to talent-focused succession planning can be more nimble and flexible, having the talent and capacity at hand to take advantage of opportunities whenever they arise. The executive's job is "doable" because leadership is shared. A talented, leader-rich staff energizes the board by providing the occasion for high-level strategy development and reassures them by demonstrating that staff leadership is broadly shared and backed up. Because the agency has developed its bench strength and backed up all key executive functions, it is ready for an executive transition whenever it might occur. The more an agency has engaged in strategic leader development, the more smoothly it will move through its leadership transitions.

Strategic leader development is typically a facet of an agency's strategic-planning process. Once strategic directions are set, the strategic-planning body details what resources are needed to pursue them, such as new revenues, programmatic restructuring, facility and technology updates, and expanded programmatic and administrative skills. A staff development plan is crafted and allocated its piece of the agency's time and money pie, which is shared, for example, with the plans for bringing in new computers, for instituting a major donor campaign, and for opening a new client service facility.

Emergency Succession Planning

A more abbreviated form of leadership development occurs when an organization undertakes *emergency succession planning,* which is a sound risk-management practice. All organizations, regardless of size, should have a board-adopted plan for emergency backup. Such planning ensures the viability of an agency in the event of the emergency absence of a key manager. With the resulting deepened talent pool, an organization can sustain services through the temporary loss of one or more administrators due to sickness, accident, or other unexpected leave. To this end, creation of an emergency succession plan is strongly recommended. An emergency succession plan template developed by CompassPoint is available in Appendix B.

The emergency planning starts with identifying the key leadership and administrative functions carried out by the executive director. Backups are then identified for each function, usually from among top managers in the agency. In a particularly small agency one of the backups might be a board member; the board treasurer would cover financial management, for instance. A cross-training plan is then crafted for the backups.

Some executives, to test the strength of their benches, have taken a leave or sabbatical once the cross-training is complete. Staff are told they can contact the executive only in the event of an emergency.

References at the end of this book can help your organization to learn more about succession planning, including departure-defined succession, strategic leader development, and emergency succession planning.

The Role of the Departing Executive

Especially complicated for a board in a transition involving a departing executive who's had an accomplished tenure is providing the incumbent the full respect he deserves while firmly coaxing him into an advisory role on the sidelines. In the ETM model, the board takes the top role in planning the agency's future and in pursuing a new leader who fits that future. The executive's advice is highly valued but not followed in all respects as the board sets a future course for the agency. This may be a new relationship dynamic for the executive and board.

A few weeks into her transition, one executive who had founded her agency fifteen years earlier complained, "I feel like I've been kicked to the curb!" Another founder, after his executive committee had met without him for the first time in his tenure, expressed his pique with the opinion that "they're acting weird!"

Emily Redington and Donn Vickers, with the Academy for Leadership and Governance in Columbus, Ohio, in their excellent booklet *Following the Leader* speak to the departing executive's final two leadership tasks as being the "leadership of letting go" and the "leadership of preparing the way." The executive can usually see the wisdom in that framing but has trouble living it.

Poor communications with your executive can result in bad blood and unintentional sabotage of the process. To prevent this, the board chair or the executive committee should talk with the executive at the outset about the roles each will play in the transition. The discussion should cover the rationale behind the board's taking control of the process, how the executive can support the board's work, and what the board can do to ease the executive's pangs at letting go. Candid and full communications from the board at each step in the process will honor the executive's position and prevent suspicions of nefarious activities from arising.

The more an executive has trouble loosening his grip on the controls, the more difficult and painful any transition process will be. The easier handoffs to successors are those in which the executive can embrace the "leadership of letting go." An executive coach can provide a safe and professional venue for the executive to talk about "control issues" and the discomfort of leaving a job that's been his life and professional identity. A board can support the use of a coach by offering to include the cost of coaching in the agency's transition budget.

Bottom line, the board needs to give extra attention to its ongoing relationship with the departing executive, whose role is central to the transition to new leadership. The unhappy executive will consciously or unconsciously be a hindrance to the work of the transition committee and be a drag on the agency's enthusiastic embrace of his successor.

A New Role for the Incumbent?

In some cases, particularly with a founder or an executive who is moving into retirement, boards may desire to have her stay with the agency in a formal role. She's been a major asset to the agency that folks would like to hold on to.

Whatever role the previous leader takes should be structured in a way that supports the leadership of the new executive and does not impinge on his prerogatives. If it's a staff role, such as director of public policy, it's under the supervision of the executive. If an emeritus role, such as founder and ambassador-at-large, the role's parameters should be set by the board and monitored by the executive. The previous executive should wait a year or more before joining the board.

And whatever the previous executive's new status, she should physically move out of the agency's facility for three months or more. The former executive's presence slows staff's detachment from the old leader and attachment to the new.

Dealing with Internal Candidates

One or more members of staff or board may apply for the executive position. The transition and search committee needs to work with these candidacies with respect and the integrity of the search process in mind.

A board member who applies should immediately leave the board, either by resigning or by taking a temporary leave. She can't be in a position to influence the process or appear to be able to do so.

Staff members who apply should also be kept at a distance from the committee's work and from staff input to the committee. For instance, when staff are discussing what attributes they'd like to see in the next executive, staff candidates should be absent.

It's a credit to the agency that there are staff who are possibly qualified to step up to the top job. It speaks to the agency's success at developing bench strength and finding talent. As internal applications are received, the committee may provide an extra degree of thanks to the applicants along with the cooler acknowledgment sent to all applicants.

The committee should avoid discussing any candidacies, internal or external, until the Prepare phase of their work is complete. At that point they will have made clear the future directions of the agency and its leadership needs. With those parameters in place, they can more objectively look at how well any candidate fits the bill.

The internal candidates' applications are considered along with the rest of the pool. If they come close to fitting the candidate profile, they should be invited to an interview. "Courtesy interviews" are generally not a good idea. If the committee sees that the candidate is clearly not qualified, or doesn't come close to measuring up to the top candidates, the courtesy interview is likely to be uncomfortable for all parties. The committee will move through it without great enthusiasm and the candidate will sense the artificiality of the situation.

A better practice is for a committee member to talk with the rejected internal candidate to discuss where she falls short, admire her ambition and desire to serve, and encourage her to work on the gaps in her resume. The candidate will appreciate the candor and encouragement. The committee will feel good about having maintained the integrity of the process.

Internal candidates heighten the need for a tight seal of confidentiality around the content of the committee's discussions. Board and staff on the committee may be in close contact with the candidates in the course of doing the agency's business. Any discussion of what's going on in the committee must remain strictly out-of-bounds.

Crafting Exit Packages

For the long-tenured executive, one going into retirement or semiretirement, a board may find it important to provide a departure package for a number of reasons. Failing to do so when the situation calls for it can make for a sour ending with the departing executive, leave key parties uneasy, and detract from an enthusiastic beginning with the succeeding executive.

The executive's annual salary may have fallen significantly below market. At one extreme, when some boards do their compensation research, they find that they need to offer 20 to 30 percent more than the retiring executive is receiving. The differential can make for an unhappy ending for the executive if it is not in some way acknowledged.

The agency may have had no retirement savings plan in place, such as a 401(k). Or it may have set it up only within the last few years. For that and other reasons, the older executive may have limited funds set aside for retirement.

The board may offer a departure package simply as acknowledgment that the executive's career earnings are modest because she chose to pursue a career of community service, rather than to apply her talents to a for-profit career that would have provided much greater lifetime earnings.

And, importantly, a financial acknowledgment for long service and career achievements may make for a more timely departure. Some executives who have privately acknowledged it's time to leave the job hang on out of financial necessity that could be eased with an exit package.

The package can take a variety of forms. There is no nonprofit industry standard or common practice. And a board may be unable to offer all that it thinks is justified because of limited resources. In some cases it will be a financial gift pegged to a certain criterion, such as two thousand dollars for each year of tenure. In others, it is a one-year consulting retainer equal to 50 percent of the executive's final annual salary. Some boards have given an expenses-paid trip to Europe for the retiree who is fond of traveling. When the package involves significant dollars, it is important to consult with an attorney versed in nonprofit law regarding any restrictions on financial bonuses or gifts that may apply.

Grooming a Successor

Grooming a successor, in theory, may seem to be a best practice to be expected of all executive directors. In reality, however, there are several pitfalls in doing so, some of which are more easily avoided than others.

A not uncommon problem arises when an "heir apparent" is named some years before the expected departure of the executive. Later, when the executive's departure is at hand, it's decided that the nominee is unsuited to be executive director. The demands of the job changed over time or he failed to live up to the expectation that he would develop the critical executive skills required.

The failure phenomenon also occurs when the hoped-for heir is hired into a deputy position because she has skills complementary to the executive's skill set. But, as many have learned, the deputy with the organizational skills to "keep the trains running on time" may be unsuited in temperament and skills to step into the role of creative visionary and builder of external relationships. The rejected heir, whose organizational skills are important to the agency, is likely to leave.

In another failed version, the successor title is not publicly given to the deputy, but the executive has privately undertaken to groom him to succeed. Sometime later, as the executive gives the board a six-month notice of leave, the executive states that she has prepared the deputy to step into the job. The board, previously unaware of the succession plan, declares itself dubious that the deputy is right for the job. It decides the deputy should compete against other candidates generated by a full-blown search. A power struggle between board and executive ensues.

There may well be a potential successor known to the executive of an agency. If so, the executive, as early as possible, should engage the board in the decision to prepare the possible heir. The board should set skill demands in line with the strategic directions of the agency. Board and executive can establish performance benchmarks to be met by the future candidate in the years leading up to the leadership transition. Finally, the board should set a deadline for the decision to go with the groomed candidate or to open up an external search.

This inclusive grooming approach usually works if the executive leaves on schedule. The executive who decides to stay longer than originally projected risks losing the successor, who likely will pursue another executive job rather than hang around indefinitely.

Grooming a successor may be a means of maintaining the status quo. Preparing an heir should be weighed against the benefits of opening the job up to external candidates with a fresh perspective on the work of the agency and a different set of skills than the incumbent. The established, "institutional" agency, such as the local Red Cross chapter, may be well served in bringing on an internally groomed successor. A younger agency, or an older one that is experiencing significant growth in a dynamic environment, may want to look for a leader with the skills to expand the enterprise beyond the capacity and breadth of vision reached by the incumbent.

Embracing Diversity and Difference

According to surveys, the current cohort of nonprofit executives is overwhelmingly white, non-Hispanic. However, our communities and the constituencies our nonprofit agencies serve have grown dramatically diverse over the past few decades. Put simply, most current nonprofit leaders do not look like the people they serve.

One critical opportunity in setting strategic directions during the Prepare phase is looking toward building the cultural competency of the agency and the diversity of its talent pool. What does the agency need to do to better connect with the cultures of its clientele and to reflect the demographics of the communities served? This will involve strategies at the board level and in staff recruitment and talent development. The candidate profile should then include skills at forming and implementing the strategies.

Board members and staff leaders must challenge their preconceptions about what leadership talent looks like. To what degree are they open to having a leader with a background and culture different from their own or different from that of the current executive? What challenges would a minority leader face stepping into an organization that may be unconsciously steeped in the ways of mainstream culture?

In recruiting, some organizations will set a target number for qualified candidates representing various constituencies. The search stays open until the target is reached, ensuring a diverse candidate pool.

Creating a multicultural organization is hard work, best done incrementally over time. The task is more than one of diversifying staff demographics. It entails tough changes, moving beyond doing business the way it's always been done. The board that hires a person of color into an established agency whose staff and board are largely white, without attention to the dynamics of the agency that will resist cultural change, may well be setting the new executive up for failure.

Using an Interim Executive Director

If the departing executive is giving less than four months' notice, the board will need to consider the appointment of a temporary executive to avoid rushing the ETM process. An internal manager may be able to step up; a board member may have the skills and time to lead the agency for a bit; or an external candidate may be sought.

In deciding who's best suited for the interim assignment, the board should first take stock of the transition needs of the agency. If programs are running smoothly, the finances are in good order, and there are no major challenges on the horizon, an internal candidate may fit the bill. If a current staff person is going to be asked to step up, that person's ability to supervise his peers for a bit and then to return to peer status should be evaluated. If you consider a board candidate, avoid the temptation to consider board experience as sufficient preparation for the executive role, particularly if you've had a competent executive in place. The job may look easier from the board perch than it is on the ground. The board should vet the board volunteer for her management experience and for her understanding of nonprofit dynamics, such as staff expectation that decision making will be inclusive. The board should take care that the board member who temporarily takes the reins can return to a governance relationship with the next regular executive and avoid the temptation to micromanage her.

To take full advantage of the transformative opportunities during the transition period, an agency is usually best served by an interim executive director who has embraced the concepts underpinning the ETM model. The best interim leader comes in not only to hold the reins for a few months but also to partner with the board—and with the transition consultant who may be in place—to move staff and program toward the "new beginning" with the permanent executive who will be arriving soon.[15]

The temporary executive best situated to lead change is more likely to come from outside the agency. Internal staff and board are steeped in the current ways and means of doing business. The externally recruited interim executive brings a fresh, objective perspective to the agency, a perspective that helps the agency take stock and update its strategic directions.

An agency that is in turnaround mode or faces problems with its programs or funding should definitely recruit a skilled interim executive. The previous executive may have been terminated and left some major messes behind. Staff morale may be in the pits. Or financial management systems may be seriously deficient. Bringing on a properly skilled interim leader to address those needs immediately will result in an agency that's more attractive to potential permanent candidates. It's also going to free the next executive to pursue the agency's future directions rather than repairing problems from the past.

As an important adjunct to its ETM services, CompassPoint maintains a pool of candidates available for interim executive positions in the San Francisco Bay Area. We require that any member of the pool has substantial experience as a nonprofit executive director. We match the skills of interim with the client agency's capacity-building needs. Similar temporary placement services are available in a few other cities, typically managed by the local nonprofit management support organization.[16] Candidates can also be found via some informal networking. One source might be a foundation that currently funds you; your program officer may know of veteran executives who could fill your need. Or your United Way will have a list of nonprofit consultants, some of whom also take on interim executive assignments.

Beyond addressing immediate capacity-building needs in a transition period, an interim leader provides the time needed for a "good ending" with the previous executive, enabling a "good beginning" with the next permanent executive.[17]

Use of an interim executive can be a critical strategy in a transition from the "long and strong" executive, as described in the succession-planning section earlier in this chapter. Anecdotes abound in the nonprofit sector about the short and troubled tenures of executives who immediately succeed long-term directors, especially directors who founded their agencies. The immediate successors become the "unintentional interims," derailed by inadequate attention to having complete and "good endings" with the predecessors. The interim executive who addresses these dynamics prepares the way for a successful entry by the next permanent executive.

Sometimes, it's a short-term executive who is leaving a lot of unhappy staff or board members behind. In these cases, the agency still may benefit from an interim executive. A cooling-off period can decrease the likelihood that the next executive is not ambushed by staff acting out conscious or unconscious resentments generated by the predecessor's tenure.

A skilled interim leader can dramatically up the chances that you will have a successful start to the next executive's tenure. The time allows the agency to take full advantage of the transformative opportunities in an executive transition process.

Choosing and Using Consultants and Recruiters

The author hopes that this guide will enable many boards to successfully and efficiently manage leadership transitions in their agencies without engaging outside consultants or recruiters.

If your organization has recently updated its strategic plan, has a high-performing set of programs, and is operating in a relatively stable environment, it can move through the phases of a transition without outside help. The participation of a board member who has experience leading staff transitions in a nonprofit setting will still be very helpful. With self-led transitions, a board member who has ample time to oversee the steps detailed in this guide should chair the transition committee. He needs to be both a skilled meeting facilitator and a good project manager, keeping tasks on schedule.

Boards use outside help for a variety of reasons:

- ▶ The agency appears prepared for a smooth transition, but no one on the board really has enough time to lead the process.
- ▶ The board may feel competent in the search and screening but would really like to have expert guidance in arriving at updated strategic directions during the Prepare phase of the work.
- ▶ Even with ample person power on the board, it prefers to have a coach for advice and problem solving while the board does most all of the work.
- ▶ The board knows there are likely big and only vaguely specified changes ahead for the agency, for which a consultant's guidance and legwork are essential.
- ▶ The board is excited by the transformational possibilities in leadership transition and wants an experienced transition pro to help make the most of the opportunities.

Choose a consultant or recruiter who cares about nonprofit capacity-building—who sees the transformational possibilities in leadership turnovers. You're looking for much more than a quick recruitment and screening process. Both skills and chemistry are important. Price is a factor for most boards; it pays to comparison shop.

Your consultant must know what it takes to be the executive director in resource-strapped nonprofit cultures, which have some norms significantly different from those in the corporate world. For instance, the executive, outside of crisis management, is generally expected to exercise "legislative power" to facilitate staff toward agency goals as opposed to "position power."[18] Staff rewards are different. Salaries alone are usually not enough to retain staff; they're seeking other payoffs as well, such as seeing homeless clients move into permanent housing or seeing to the construction of low-income housing as a means of preventing homelessness.

As previously noted, you may well be able to get special funding to pay for consultant services from one of your agency's current funders. Foundations that have invested funds in your programs are often willing to support transition and search assistance. They are as concerned that your services continue in good stead as you are, and they will be impressed with your board's diligence in managing the transition. You can save time by seeking funds while simultaneously interviewing potential consultants.

To generate candidates to meet your consulting need, you might start with an Internet search for "transition consultant" or "nonprofit search consultant." (The concept of "transition consultant" is still new and not prevalent in many communities.) Funders, the United Way, other boards, and colleagues at other nonprofits are all excellent sources.

In a best-case scenario, two or three consulting candidates will be interviewed by a board committee (the executive committee, if the transition committee has not yet been formed) to check for skills and fit. The consultants will also want an opportunity to check out whether they believe their skills are a fit for your needs. Questions you might ask include the following:

▷ Tell us about your approach to managing executive transitions.

▷ How would you go about helping us clarify our strategic directions?

▷ Where would you find talented candidates for our executive position?

▷ How many agencies of our size and in our business line have you assisted?

▷ What would you do, and what would you expect us to do, in this process?

▷ What are your conditions for success in a consulting engagement?

▷ What do you need to know about us before making a decision to consult on our executive transition?

▷ If we need to bring on an interim executive director while we're working with you, how might you help us to do that?

▷ What is your fee structure? Can you give us a ballpark estimate on what the total cost of your contract with us would be?

▷ Are you acquainted with any of our major funders?

▷ Please give us three references for your work with nonprofits.

It's best if the interviews can be conducted in one sitting, with the committee having time at the end of the interviews to discuss their impressions and to make a decision on the consultant from which it wants to request a contract proposal. While the preferred consultant is putting together a contract proposal tailored to your needs, the committee should check references. The committee chair may be empowered to negotiate the final terms of the contract after it is received from the consultant.

As the consulting work begins, it's good practice to schedule periodic feedback sessions between the committee chair and the consultant. Is the consultant living up to the terms of the contract? Are both parties adhering to the conditions for success? Have conditions within the agency been identified that require more work or different work from the consultant, requiring a contract amendment? Regular check-ins on the progress of the work should provide for course corrections that ensure successful outcomes and prevent after-the-fact dissatisfactions on either side.

▲ ▲ ▲

We hope Chapter Six gives you some additional insights into the many nuances of the transition process. If you have a solid organization with straightforward transition needs, you may need to adjust your plan only minimally, if at all. If you need to factor into your process a number of the issues outlined above, you now have a stronger, richer transition plan that nips some problems in the bud. In either case, you are going into this crucial process well prepared, with your eyes wide open.

Afterword

An executive transition can be a daunting time for an organization, but when handled well and thoughtfully, it can be a major opportunity for your organization and set you on a path for long-term success.

This book has presented a model that has been used by hundreds of nonprofits over the past decade in taking advantage of the opportunities presented by their leadership turnovers. The ETM process begins with the Prepare phase in gathering and analyzing data on your agency's achievements to date and challenges going forward. The end products are an exciting leadership agenda that sets clear strategies for growing your mission impact and a candidate profile that spells out the kind of executive director you need to pursue that agenda. Two streams of activity occur in the succeeding Pivot phase: the aggressive recruitment and careful screening of a pool of candidates who fit the candidate profile and a start on some of the operational upgrades that are highlighted as needed by your agency in the leadership agenda. The Thrive phase begins with the thoughtful installation of your newly hired executive, a set of steps that assure she is clear on what you expect her to achieve and that she has the productive connections with board, staff, and community that will set her and your agency up for success in pursuing your strategic aspirations.

There is probably no one agency that has ever used every ingredient in this book's ETM recipe in moving through its executive transition. Each board and nonprofit agency adapt the recipe according to their tastes and to the time, talent, and money they have at hand. However, when enough of the ingredients are carefully blended into your transition by a committee excited by the chance to cook up something great for your agency's future, the outcome can be a delight for all parties—as the personal story below demonstrates.

I recently completed work with a large community mental health agency whose highly regarded executive of thirty years was leaving his position on six months' notice. The staff, from top managers to frontline caseworkers, was highly anxious in being faced with losing a leader who had created an agency culture of respect and caring for staff and clients alike. The liaisons in the various government and foundation funding agencies were nervous about the loss of a mental health visionary who had deftly managed a complex web of revenue streams in supporting a broad set of mental health services critical to the community. The board, passionate about the mental health mission of the agency, was anxious as well. But some board leaders also had glimmers of the opportunity to build on the executive's achievements that the transition presented.

The board chair headed the transition committee that included two additional board members and three staff. The committee saw not only the advantages of going through the Prepare phase at a deliberate pace but also the necessity, if the agency were to avoid a misstep or a bad hire that could result in a downturn with the executive's departure. They dedicated six weeks to data gathering and analysis, collecting information from funders, peer agencies, staff, and board members. The resulting leadership agenda included a vision for significantly expanding the agency's client capacity across a three-county region and strategies for raising the funds to do so. The agenda also spoke to the agency's need to better document its client outcomes, an imperative highlighted by the agency's funders.

The executive's downloading to his managers of his knowledge and management strategies, especially with regard to finances and contract management, was a key Pivot activity. A national search ensued for candidates with the skills and experience indicated by the leadership agenda. The candidate screening process was extensive, with the committee narrowing the applicants down to two impressive finalists. Among other activities, these finalists had interviews with staff and with the outgoing executive before their interviews with the board. The board was unanimous in making a choice and negotiated a solid employment agreement with the new executive, who has started work on growing the agency's revenues and client capacity.

In feedback on the executive transition process the board led, the staff expressed enormous gratitude for having been included throughout the three phases. It gave them enthusiasm for working with the new executive and a sense of relief that the agency would continue to be a great place to work and to pursue their personal passions for being of service to the community. The board is particularly excited with the prospect of serving more community members in need of their services and of being involved in the fundraising that will make the expansion possible. And the funding agencies are relieved that an agency important to their community missions will maintain and even grow its work.

The author's goal with this book is to give you tools you can use in guiding your agency to a successful transition not unlike that achieved by the organization highlighted in the personal story above. My hope is that your agency will be infused with excitement for the future of its important community work as a result.

Appendix A:

Stepping Up: A Board's Challenge in Leadership Transition

by Tim Wolfred
© 2002 CompassPoint Nonprofit Services

Note: This article is reprinted from CompassPoint Nonprofit Services.
It originally appeared in The Nonprofit Quarterly, *vol. 9, no. 4.*
www.nonprofitquarterly.org.

When the executive director steps down, the board has to step up and take charge in ways that may be new to it. In consulting with over one hundred nonprofits in transition, we've seen that nothing has greater impact on the outcome than a board's leadership skills in exploiting the moment of leadership turnover for its myriad opportunities.

Minimally, a board hopes to lose no ground in handing the agency keys to a new director. But beyond maintaining the status quo, transitions offer unique opportunities for renewal and growth. Whether ground is gained, held, or lost depends largely on the board. There's real work to be done for the good of your mission, work more complicated than simple recruiting, as the board makes several key decisions: What is our vision for this agency? How well do current operations fit that vision? What kind of person can implement that vision while competently addressing our operational needs? How are we going to recruit? Are we ready to guide and support our new executive?

A board must communicate with key constituencies, particularly staff and funders, during transition. These stakeholders are deeply invested in your mission and usually more than a bit nervous when your leader resigns—you must ensure their confidence in your approach to the transition.

If your board is organized around a strong executive, you have tricky dynamics of power shifting. How does the board respectfully take the reins and put them squarely into the hands of the next executive? The board's challenge is to exercise its own power thoughtfully while honoring the legacy of the departing exec and helping to transfer knowledge and influence from the exiting to the entering leader.

Following is some of what we have learned about what the board must attend to during a transition. At the end of the article and on page 143 are suggestions about types of help you may wish to employ in facing these issues.

Pleasure and Pain

As with most significant change, executive transitions can cause both pleasure and pain.

Taking the time in the transition to create a fresh vision and to consider new ways of working generates excitement. But you must also take stock of where you are currently. In many cases a candid assessment of an agency's strengths and weaknesses can cause serious discomfort. There may be intense struggles as competing opinions emerge on how to address deficiencies and on setting future directions—all part of a healthy process essential to capacity building.

Complicating the mix is the departing executive director, who wants the best for the agency's future but may dread a board looking into the closets. Even the best executive directors know they could have carried out some duties better if they'd had enough time and resources. They worry their legacy of achievements may be tarnished if the board pushes to shed light on organizational shortcomings developed or not resolved on their watch. It is the board's delicate job to understand this very human fear and to remain supportive both of the executive director and of the daylight shedding.

> **An Inspirational Tale:** Recently I warned a board president and a good friend that she was in for a bumpy ride with the transition of her executive director. She called to thank me for my warning—the bumps would have been harder to take if she hadn't expected them. The board had navigated the stormy seas in airing the issues that needed to be addressed. They also helped the executive work through his ambivalence about leaving, expressed in two temporary reversals of his resignation decision. Additionally there had been heated meetings where

the board managed to thwart a drive to anoint an internal successor without a search.

To avoid pain, some boards will neglect airing the problems—especially when they've enjoyed working with a creative, strong executive. Maybe the executive has done a particularly good job bringing in money or has through strength of personality and character gained the agency prestige. In such cases, a board may be eager to accept at face value the executive's declarations that things are generally fine and all that's needed is to find a successor who can continue along the same path. At other times the board is glad to have the executive leave and just wants the transition to end as quickly and easily as possible.

But failure to examine an agency's operations with due diligence not only misses a key growth opportunity, it also can set up the successor for trouble that can lead to a short tenure.

> **A Cautionary Tale:** One agency recently lost its new executive after several troubled months. In 10 years, his predecessor had doubled the agency's size and forged important collaborations with government funders. But the staff, 25 strong, had chafed under his imperious management style; turnover was high. Unaware of the staff turmoil, the board hired a similarly autocratic leader.
>
> Additionally, staff and board were predominantly white, serving a client population 90 percent people of color. Although the board recognized this issue, it simply charged the new executive with diversifying the staff, without itself studying the issue.

The mix of angry staff, brash new executive, and fiats on diversifying was explosive. The new executive was in constant conflict with his staff. The board was frustrated and baffled about what had gone wrong. Funding fell off. The executive director resigned. The agency now struggles to recover.

Communicate, Communicate, Communicate

A board must check in with key stakeholders early and often in the course of a transition.

Staff Input

Staff are often those most unsettled by an executive turnover. They may have bonded with the personality, vision, and administrative ways of your executive director—or at least they've adjusted to her ways in order to do the work they want to do for your clients. They need time to come to terms with her departure and they will be anxious about how the next leader will approach the work.

Staff needs to see that the board is leading a thoughtful transition to new leadership. For example, it's helpful for the board president to visit a staff meeting to hear staff concerns and discuss the transition plan—this physical presence is a powerful acknowledgment of the importance of staff issues.

No board examination of an agency's health is complete without the staff's perspective. We use a brief, anonymous staff survey to elicit useful information on agency operations. It includes these two questions: What barriers to your doing your job well exist at the agency? What are the barriers to the agency achieving its mission? Any perceived barrier mentioned by at least three staff gets further investigation. (The same survey honors the legacy of the departing executive director with a request to list her top three achievements and asks which of her leadership skills are important for her successor to possess.)

> **Staff Versus Management Perceptions:** We interviewed the 10 top managers in a 60-person health services agency where we were doing an interim directorship. On the barriers question, they identified infrastructure needs (better facilities, updated computer systems), and the need for more aggressive outreach. The managers reported staff productivity and morale as high.
>
> The staff survey, however, drew a different picture. Half of the respondents reported poor supervisory support as a barrier to their success, among additional managerial problems. When the data was presented to the managers, they decided with the interim executive director to boost their managerial skills with a professional development plan.

Including staff representatives on the board's transition committee can provide critical perspectives on future directions and what is needed in the next executive. In the final selection phase, a chance for staff to meet the candidates from whom the board will choose their next boss provides excellent information, and further cements staff buy-in and loyalty to whomever is hired.

Funders as Information Resources

The second key constituency with whom you must skillfully communicate is your donors and government and foundation program officers. They may fund your operations not only because they are committed to your mission but also because they trust your agency's leader. News of that leader's departure may give them pause. They may have also observed problems with leadership and been unsure of how to communicate them. A letter detailing the board's transition plan—and phone calls to the top tier of supporters—softens concerns and helps to hold their trust.

Additionally, funders not only know your agency and have ideas on how it might improve, they also have perspective on the broader nonprofit environment. A program officer who's giving grants to you and to several related agencies can tell you about funding trends and about programmatic innovations in your field. Also, she may know of experienced professionals in your sector who are possible candidates. It is always worth inviting funders to invest in the transition process, but bill it as the pivotal capacity building moment it really is!

> **The Bigger Picture:** The executive director of an agency working with homeless mothers and children was moving overseas. In five years the executive had dramatically raised the quality of the agency's programs. Staff in all divisions reported high job satisfaction and pride in being part of the innovative programs. Funders and peer agencies unanimously praised the agency's success.
>
> Foundation and government supporters also talked of the upcoming "regionalization" of Bay Area services to homeless families. The only housing affordable for San Francisco families moving out of homelessness is a county or two away. Future contracts would go to agencies capable of following their clients into their new, and distant, housing. This would mean opening offices close to affordable housing or collaborating with agencies in other counties. The board decided the next executive director had to address regionalization. They moved from wanting to hire a "clone" of their revered director to pursuing a different set of skills.

Preparing the Way

In an excellent booklet on the departures of nonprofit founders, Redington and Vickers[19] frame the executive's final two leadership tasks as "letting go" and "preparing the way" for a successor. Often a critical board task, then, is to support their executive director through these final duties.

Successful execs rarely let go easily. Essential to their achievements have been their passion for your mission and the energy they've devoted to the work. How do they now coolly detach and trust that the enterprise, for which they've given and sacrificed so much, will not suffer for their leaving?

A board inattentive to the personal struggle in letting go may find the transition derailed by an ambivalent, anxious departing executive "acting out." We've seen resignations withdrawn after serious transition planning has begun, resistance to a full audit of administrative records, demands to choose the successor, insistence on being part of every step of recruiting and selection, and criticisms of the board's transition work to staff, colleagues, and even funders.

It's up to the board to bring a healthy, clear closure to the tenure of the incumbent by, among other things, acknowledging his legacy with receptions and written testimonials by staff, funders, clients, and board. Feeling appreciated, outgoing executive directors are emotionally freer to help prepare the way for a successor.

Usually the executive director should be an advisor—not the captain—in the transition. A board's first search task is to assess current challenges and future vision for the agency, then to build its profile of the skills and characteristics needed in the next executive director. Too much guidance from the departing executive director can cause organizational challenges to be overlooked and can too strongly shape the vision around the exiting executive director's sensibilities. The board alone has full responsibility in making the choice and making sure their choice succeeds. Too heavy a reliance on the judgment of the previous executive in screening and hiring weakens the board's commitment to the next executive director as their own. Literally and figuratively, the executive director should not be in the room as the board chooses their next executive.

The executive director should not anoint a successor—at least not without the board independently deciding what the successor needs to look like—and the smart successor will want to have been chosen first and foremost by the board, his or her future working partner. It's dangerous for the agency and the next executive director if the board evades an arduous choice by letting another authority choose.

Finally, the board needs to clarify what role the departing exec wants to play with the agency in the future. Help with fundraising? Be a goodwill ambassador for the agency with important stakeholders? Focus on policy with key decision-makers? Whatever the role, the board must set limits so his presence empowers the successor. An unfettered, overly involved predecessor can so dominate a successor that the new executive director is never fully in control (or, worse, is seriously undermined), making her tenure frustrating and often short.

Two More Cautionary Tales: An executive director of a youth services agency, who had been on the job for six months, called me for advice. She said that her predecessor, although off the payroll, was still occupying her old office in the agency—and regularly offering advice on all matters. We talked about how the caller could convince her board of the need to step in and move the predecessor out of the building.

The charismatic founder of a health advocacy agency left the executive director job after two years. He did not have the skills or desire to be chief administrator of what had quickly developed into a successful policy and prevention program. A new executive director was hired. The founder moved out and was put on retainer for fundraising and speechmaking, but he couldn't relinquish control. He remained socially close to the activist staff, most of whom he had directly hired. When the new executive director set a direction he did not agree with, he organized staff to resist. Two years into the successor's rocky term, staff went into full rebellion and the executive director resigned. The next hire set clear terms of engagement with the founder before accepting the job. The board agreed to enforce the terms.

A continuing relationship with a departing executive can be worked out, but it is tricky enough that we advise you to set limits. There are many cases where everyone smiles smugly in a "we are all mature enough to handle this" way before the transition, only to become immersed in horribly awkward interactions that retard progress and distract focus.

Success with the New Hire

Diligently moving through a productive close with the departing executive director and a demanding search and screening can exhaust a board. The temptation is to hand the new hire the keys and slip away for a rest. But skipping the final phase can set up a board for unnecessary trouble.

Yet More Cautionary Tales: One exec tells of his board being so depleted when he started that they couldn't muster a quorum for his first five board meetings. Faced with revenue short-falls due to tough economic times, he had to restructure services, cutting two staff positions, all without serious board discussion. He's now feeling stressed and isolated, and considering resignation.

In another agency, the founder built an innovative, successful youth service program in an inner-city neighborhood. The board envisioned replicating it in several other neighborhoods. To that end, they hired a private sector entrepreneur to succeed the founder. He had served on several nonprofit boards but had not worked in a community agency. They turned him loose, and six months later complaints were coming from staff and funders. He was running afoul of an agency culture that had valued staff input. His aggressive expansion tactics, which complainants asserted were more appropriate to the competitive business world than to a collaborative nonprofit environment, were repelling community supporters.

We recommend that a board establish a fresh orientation and support committee to succeed the typically exhausted search committee in installing the new executive. The first day on the job, for instance, the board president introduces the new hire to staff, highlighting the qualifications that made him stand out among the candidates, and thanking staff for their help in the transition.

The committee details an initial set of explicit executive director performance goals based on major agency objectives. Some weeks later, they revisit the goals for possible changes based on the executive director's newly grounded perspective on what's possible.

The committee sets up the "social contract" between the executive director and the board, stating the kind of help they expect from each other, including formal and informal protocols for communications. The committee helps the executive director craft a support and development plan.

People hired by mid- to small-sized agencies are often new to the executive director role and can profit from structured help in their complex and demanding jobs; we suggest an executive coach or mentor, classes on management skills, or a peer support group for guidance and empathy.

Getting Ready and Getting Help

Most boards manage transitions with internal resources: a search committee, perhaps a staff manager for input and administrative support. The committee chair is a board officer with experience in hiring professional staff, and the time to oversee a transition.

The committee seeks external and internal perspectives on the agency's challenges and future. Several committee members devote time to aggressive recruitment, carefully vetting resumes and then candidates. The committee sends two or three finalists to the board, which makes a choice and delegates the installation of its new executive to a board member or two.

A board short on experience or hours for the transition tasks may contract with a consultant. Our contracts at CompassPoint have ranged from 30 hours for limited coaching of a board to 300 hours providing most of the labor required in a transition.

Money can be a barrier to asking for assistance; however, most of our clients have gotten grants from their funders to cover all or some of their transition costs. Many foundations are pleased when asked for transition help, because they already have a stake in your making the right hire. A modest one-time grant to help you through the process protects that investment.

Admittedly, I may be biased by the fact that transition work with nonprofits is my business, but I believe almost every board, when possible, is wise to seek the objectivity of an experienced consultant for their leadership transition. The work can be tough and the pitfalls numerous. Expert guidance and facilitation can save time, ease a board through the rough spots, and help it explore the renewal opportunities in a transition. You may want to avoid the expense, but the cost of missed opportunities—or of failure—can be much higher.

Appendix B:

Emergency Succession-Planning Template

▷ All nonprofit agencies should have an emergency succession plan to cover the sudden and unexpected absences of their executive directors. This sample plan is modeled on an actual plan. In this model, special emphasis is given to identifying the key leadership functions carried by the executive, identifying the agency managers best qualified to step into the executive role in an emergency, and prescribing the cross-training necessary to prepare the backup managers to cover the leadership functions. One major side benefit to implementing this plan is a management team with enhanced leadership skills.

Emergency Succession Plan

(Agency Name)

This plan provides a procedure for the appointment of an acting executive director in the event of an unplanned absence of the executive director.

1. Rationale

In order to ensure the continuous coverage of executive duties critical to the ongoing operations of *(Agency Name)* and its services to clients, the board of directors is adopting policies and procedures for the temporary appointment of an acting executive director in the event of an *unplanned and extended absence* of the executive director.

While the board acknowledges that such an absence is highly improbable and certainly undesirable, it also believes that due diligence in exercising its governance functions requires that it have an emergency executive succession plan in place. It is expected that this plan will ensure continuity in external relationships and in staff functioning.

2. Priority functions of the executive director position at *(Agency Name)*

   The full executive director position description is attached.

   Among the duties listed in the position description, the following key functions of the executive director will be covered by an acting director:

   a. Serve as the organization's principal leader, representative, and spokesperson to the greater community.

   b. Support the board of directors.

   ▶ Ensure integrity and strength of board leadership and address issues around clarity of role, governance, bylaws or policies, corporate structure, and membership.

   ▶ Assist with recruitment and orientation of new board members.

   ▶ Prepare executive reports to board of directors and executive committee and attend various committee meetings.

   c. Convene and lead the management team.

   d. Participate in the recruitment, interview, selection, and evaluation process for directly supervised staff and other key executive-level positions.

   e. Strategize the organization's short- and long-range program and project goals.

   ▶ Identify overall resource development goals and fundraising plan.

   ▶ Establish, maintain, and cultivate relations with donors, foundations, and other resources to support organizational programs and activities.

   ▶ Maintain accountability for current-year operating budget and for financial performance of portfolio.

3. Succession plan in event of a **temporary, unplanned absence—SHORT TERM**

   a. Definitions.

   ▶ A temporary absence is one in which it is expected that the executive director will return to his position once the events precipitating the absence are resolved.

- An unplanned absence is one that arises unexpectedly, in contrast to a planned leave, such as a vacation or a sabbatical.

- A short-term absence is three months or less.

b. Who may appoint the acting executive director.

- The board of directors authorizes the executive committee to implement the terms of this emergency plan in the event of the unplanned absence of the executive director.

- In the event of an unplanned absence of the executive director, the deputy director shall immediately inform the chair of the executive committee of the absence.

- As soon as is feasible, the board chair shall convene a meeting of the executive committee to affirm the procedures prescribed in this plan or to make modifications the committee deems appropriate.

c. Standing appointee to the position of acting executive director.

- The position description of the deputy director specifies that she shall serve as acting executive director in the absence of the executive director.

d. First and second backups for the position of acting executive director.

- Should the deputy director be unable to serve as acting executive director, the first backup appointee will be the program director. The second backup appointee will be chief financial officer.

- In the event the standing appointee, the deputy director, is new to the deputy position and fairly inexperienced with *(Agency Name),* the executive committee may decide to appoint one of the backup appointees to the acting executive position. The executive committee may also consider the option of splitting executive duties among the designated appointees.

e. Cross-training plan for appointees.

- The executive director, with assistance from the deputy director, shall develop a plan for training the three potential appointees in each of the priority functions of the executive director that are listed in section 2, above. The training plan will be attached to this document when the plan is completed. The director of human resources shall have the responsibility of handling the logistics of the plan's implementation.

  f. Authority and restrictions of the appointee.

  ▸ The person appointed as acting executive director shall have the full authority for decision making and independent action as the regular executive director.

  g. Compensation.

  ▸ The acting executive director shall receive a temporary salary increase to the entry level salary of the executive director position or to 5 percent above his or her current salary, whichever is greater.

  h. Board committee responsible for oversight and support to the acting executive director.

  ▸ As with the executive director, the executive committee of the board will have responsibility for monitoring the work of the acting executive director. The executive committee will also be alert to the special support needs of the executive in this temporary leadership role.

  i. Communications plan.

  ▸ As soon as possible after the acting executive director has begun covering an unplanned absence, board members and the acting executive shall communicate the temporary leadership structure to the following key supporters external to *(Agency Name)*:

  - Government contract officers (list)
    .

    .

  - Foundation program officers (list)
    .

    .

  - Civic leaders (list)
    .

    .

  - Major donors (list)
    .

    .

4. Succession plan in event of a **temporary, unplanned absence—LONG TERM.**
  a. Definition.

  ▸ A long-term absence is one that is expected to last more than three months.

b. Procedures.

▸ The procedures and conditions to be followed shall be the same as for a short-term absence *with the addition that* the executive committee will give immediate consideration, in consultation with the acting executive director, to temporarily filling the management position left vacant by the acting executive director. This is in recognition of the fact that, for a term of more than three months, it may not be reasonable to expect the acting executive director to carry the duties of both positions. The position description of a temporary manager would focus on covering the priority areas in which the acting executive director needs assistance.

5. Succession plan in event of a **PERMANENT unplanned absence.**

a. Definition.

▸ A permanent absence is one in which it is firmly determined that the executive director will not be returning to the position.

b. Procedures.

▸ The procedures and conditions shall be the same as for a long-term temporary absence *with the addition that* the board of directors shall appoint a transition and search committee to plan and carry out a transition to a new permanent executive director.

6. Approvals and maintenance of records.

a. Succession-plan approval.

▸ This succession plan will be approved by the executive committee and forwarded to the full board of directors for its vote and approval.

b. Signatories.

▸ This plan shall be signed by the board president, the executive director, the human resources administrator, and the appointees designated in this plan.

c. Maintenance of record.

▸ Copies of this plan shall be maintained by the board president, the executive director, the deputy director, the two backup appointees, the human resources department, and the *(Agency Name)* corporate attorney.

©CompassPoint Nonprofit Services, San Francisco, CA

Appendix C:
Resources

Web Sites

The following web sites offer a number of publications (from brief thought pieces to full-length books) related directly to the executive transitions process; some also include downloadable tools that could be used by a transition and search committee:

BoardSource: www.BoardSource.org. BoardSource increases the effectiveness of nonprofit organizations by strengthening boards of directors through their consulting practice, publications, tools, and membership program.

Bridgestar: www.bridgestar.org. Bridgestar's mission is to support and strengthen nonprofit organizations by enhancing the flow and effectiveness of passionate and highly skilled leaders into and within the nonprofit sector.

CompassPoint Nonprofit Services: www.CompassPoint.org. CompassPoint is a consulting, research, and training organization providing nonprofits with management tools, strategies, and resources to lead change in their communities. With offices in San Francisco and Silicon Valley, CompassPoint works with community-based nonprofits in executive transition, planning, boards of directors, finance systems, business planning, fundraising, and technology.

execSearches.com: www.execSearches.com. execSearches.com is an online source for recruiting mid-level and executive professionals in the nonprofit, education, health care, and government sectors.

Opportunity Knocks: www.OpportunityKnocks.org. Opportunity Knocks is a national online job site focused exclusively on the nonprofit community.

TransitionsGuides: www.TransitionGuides.com. TransitionGuides is a consulting and educational services company that enables organizations to capitalize on opportunities that come with transitions.

Bibliography

Albert, Sheila. *Hiring the Chief Executive: A Practical Guide to the Search and Selection Process.* Washington, DC: BoardSource, 2000.

Annie E. Casey Foundation. *Executive Transition Monographs* (Series), http://www.aecf.org/KnowledgeCenter/PublicationsSeries/ExecutiveTransitionMonographs.aspx

Adams, Tom. "Founder Transitions: Creating Good Endings and New Beginnings," 2005.

Adams, Tom. "Stepping Up, Staying Engaged: Succession Planning and Executive Transition Management for Nonprofit Boards of Directors," 2006.

Kunreuther, Frances. "Up Next: Generation Change and the Leadership of Nonprofit Organizations," 2005.

Kunreuther, Frances, and Patrick Corvington. "Next Shift: Beyond the Nonprofit Leadership Crisis," 2008.

TransitionGuides & CompassPoint Nonprofit Services. "Capturing the Power of Leadership Change: Using Executive Transition Management to Strengthen Organizational Capacity," 2004.

Wolfred, Tim. "Building Leaderful Organizations: Succession Planning for Nonprofits," 2008.

Wolfred, Tim. "Interim Executive Directors: The Power in the Middle," 2005.

Axelrod, Nancy R. *Chief Executive Succession Planning: The Board's Role in Securing Your Organization's Future.* Washington, DC: BoardSource, 2002.

Bridges, William. *Managing Transitions: Making the Most of Change.* Reading, MA: Addison-Wesley Publishing Company, 1991.

Carlson, Mim, and Margaret Donohoe. *The Executive Director's Survival Guide: Thriving as a Nonprofit Leader.* Hoboken, NJ: Wiley & Sons, 2003.

Cornelius, Marla, Patrick Covington, and Albert Ruesga. *Ready to Lead? Next Generation Leaders Speak Out.* San Francisco: CompassPoint Nonprofit Services, 2008.

Editors. *Planning for Succession: A Toolkit for Board Members and Staff of Nonprofit Arts Organizations.* Chicago: Illinois Arts Alliance, 2004.

Gilmore, Thomas. *Making a Leadership Change: How Organizations and Leaders Can Handle Leadership Transition Successfully.* Bloomington, IN: Authors Choice Press, 2003.

Gilvar, Barbara. *The Art of Hiring Leaders: A Guide for Nonprofit Organizations.* Boston: Gilvar Publications, 2006.

Linell, Deborah, Zora Radosevich, and Jonathan Spack. *The Executive Directors Guide: The Guide for Successful Nonprofit Management.* Boston: United Way of Massachusetts Bay, 2002.

Redington, Emily, and Donn Vickers. *Following the Leader: A Guide for Planning Founding Director Transition. Leadership Report No. 1.* Columbus, OH: The Academy for Leadership and Governance, 2001.

Stevens, Susan Kenny. "Helping Founders Succeed." *Grantmakers in the Arts Newsletter* 10, no. 2 (Autumn 1999).

Wolfred, Tim. "Stepping Up: A Board's Challenge in Leadership Transitions." *The Nonprofit Quarterly* 9, no. 4 (Winter 2002): 14–19.

Notes

1. Thomas N. Gilmore, *Making a Leadership Change: How Organizations & Leaders Can Handle Leadership Transitions Successfully* (Bloomington, IN: Author's Choice Press, 2003).

2. William Bridges, *Managing Transitions: Making the Most of Change* (Reading, MA: Addison-Wesley, 1991).

3. Jeanne Bell et al., *Daring to Lead 2006* (San Francisco: CompassPoint Nonprofit Services, 2006), 5.

4. Ibid., 5; Paige Teegarden, *Nonprofit Executive Leadership and Transitions Survey 2004* (Baltimore, MD: Annie E. Casey Foundation, 2005), 4; David Birdsel and Douglas Muzzio, *The Next Leaders: UWNYC Grantee Leadership Development and Succession Management Needs* (New York: United Way, 2003), 5; Gail Randall et al., *Executive Director Tenure and Transition in Southern New England* (Worcester, MA: New England Executive Transitions Partnership, 2004), 12.

5. A variety of "bumps" and how a board might prevent them are described in an article by the author of this guide. Tim Wolfred, "Stepping Up: A Board's Challenge in Leadership Transition," *Nonprofit Quarterly* 9, no. 4 (Winter 2002), 14–19, which is provided in Appendix A of this book.

6. Bridges, *Managing Transitions* (see n. 2).

7. Author's note: The case examples in this book are based on real organizations but names and details have been changed to hide their identities.

8. Jeanne Peters and Timothy Wolfred, *Daring to Lead: Nonprofit Executive Directors and Their Work Experience* (San Francisco: CompassPoint Nonprofit Services, 2001), 13.

9. Factors to consider when deciding whether to hire a consultant are discussed in Chapter Six. Information on working with consultants is provided in Chapter Seven.

10. A description of available assessment methods is presented in the section "Gathering Input," which starts on page 46.

11. Timothy Wolfred et al. *Leadership Lost: A Study on Executive Director Tenure and Experience* (San Francisco: CompassPoint Nonprofit Services, 1999), 15–18; Peters and Wolfred, *Daring to Lead,* 21–22.

12. Peters and Wolfred, *Daring to Lead,* 13; Wolfred, *Leadership Lost,* 10 (see n. 11).

13. As noted earlier, TransitionGuides is an executive succession-planning group located near Washington, D.C.

14. Tim Wolfred, *Building Leaderful Organizations: Succession Planning for Nonprofits* (Baltimore, MD: Annie E. Casey Foundation, 2008), 4.

15. I have written on the transformative role of the interim executive in a monograph published by the Annie E. Casey Foundation, *Interim Executive Directors: The Power in the Middle.*

16. A list of management support organizations in the United States and Canada can be accessed on the home page of the Alliance for Nonprofit Management, www.allianceonline.org.

17. The terms "good ending" and "good beginning" are used here in specific reference to the change management model of William Bridges discussed in Chapter One.

18. Jim Collins, *Good to Great for the Social Sectors* (Boulder, CO: Self-published, 2005), www.jimcollins.com.

19. Emily Redington and Donn Vickers, *Following the Leader: A Guide for Planning Founding Director Transition* (Columbus, OH: The Academy for Leadership and Governance, 2001), 16.

Index

t indicates tool

acting executive directors, 123, 149–153
Adams, Tom, 1, 23–24
agencies in decline
    described, 18
    and time frame, 25
    transition needs of, 18–19, 130
application process, setting, 70–71
assessments
    of agency needs, 42
    board of directors self-, 48*t*
    of first transition committee meeting, 44
    of new executive director, 25, 108–109,
        110*t*–113*t*, 118
    sustainability audits, 121

background checks, 90, 92
beginning phase (Bridges), 11
behavioral interviewing, 84, 85*t*
benchmarks, establishing, 54
boards of directors
    and departing executive director, 28,
        140–141, 143–145
    and emergency leadership plan, 123
    hiring decision-making meeting, 95*t*,
        96–97, 97*t*
    and leadership agenda, 56–57
    member as candidate, 35, 125–126
    member as interim executive director,
        129–130
    new executive director's assessment by, 25,
        108–109, 110*t*–113*t*, 118
    new executive director's relationship with,
        10, 29, 104, 114–115, 146
    personal story of transition, 135–137
    recruitment efforts of, 3–4, 27, 29, 72*t*,
        74*t*, 75

relinquishing management duties, 14–15
    screening of finalists, 94–96
    staff trust in, 4
    strategic directions/plans survey of, 46–47,
        47*t*
    and transition and search committee, 27
    See also communication by board of
        directors
Bridges, William
    importance of, 2
    on staff morale, 62–63
    transition phases of, 10–11, 12, 28
budgets, 42

candidate profile
    creating, 54, 55*t*, 56, 58–59
    and embracing diversity, 128–129
    relationship to strategic directions/plans,
        28, 54, 56
    sample, 60*t*
    and screening, 29
candidates
    acknowledging, 77, 79*t*
    attracting, 29, 71, 72*t*, 73, 74*t*, 75, 143
    community ties of, 76
    internal, 35, 125–126
    maintaining confidentiality of, 70–71,
        76–77, 81, 125
    pool diversity, 75–76
    promoted by departing executives, 4,
        127–128, 144
    rating, 86–87, 88*t*–89*t*
    references, 29, 82, 86
    rejection notification, 80, 87, 100, 100t,
        126
    screening, 29, 77, 78*t*, 79–81
    sources for interim executive directors, 130
    See also finalists

capacity-building
    and benchmarks, 54
    during candidate search and screening,
        61–62
    for departure of long-tenured executive
        directors, 120–123
    determining needs, 28, 42, 46–47, 47t, 49,
        52t, 53–54
case examples
    City Center Homeless Services, 16–17
    Main Street Services, 20–21
    New Beginnings, 18–19
    Treasure Island Memorial Foundation,
        14–15
change elements, described, 12
City Center Homeless Services, 16–17
clients, gathering information from, 53
communication by board of directors,
    43–44, 45t
    with departing executive director, 124
    with funders, 142–143
    importance of, 139
    with new executive director, 114–115
    with staff, 28, 141–142
community. See funders
CompassPoint Nonprofit Services, 1, 2
compensation
    exit packages, 43, 126–127
    and finalists' references, 87
    in job announcement, 70
    researching, 43
confidentiality of candidates, 70–71, 76–77,
    81, 125
consultants
    choosing, 132–133
    contract with, 42
    feedback from, 133–134
    information gathering by, 53
    reasons for using, 131–132
control issues, 123–124
courtesy interviews, 126

departing executive directors
    and board of directors, 28, 140–141,
        143–145
    candidates promoted by, 4, 127–128,
        144
    closure with, 11, 25, 28, 32, 144
    exit packages for, 43, 126–127

and orientation of new executive director,
    107
    recruitment efforts of, 75
    role of, 35–36, 94, 123–125, 144–145
    strategic directions/plans survey of, 49
    unplanned, 6–7, 123, 149–153
    See also long-tenured executive directors
departure-defined succession planning,
    120–122
diversity
    of candidate pool, 75–76
    and candidate profile, 128–129
    and comfort zones, 87
    preparing for, 143
donors
    communicating with, 43–44, 45t
    and long-tenured executive directors,
        121

emergency succession planning, 6–7, 123,
    149–153
emeritus executive directors, 122, 125
emotions, role of, 12–13
ending phase (Bridges), 10, 11, 28
evaluations. See assessments
executive directors
    acting, 123, 149–153
    and agency vision, 63
    average tenures of, 7
    feedback needs of, 109
    first-time, 14–15, 25
    sudden departure of, 6–7, 123, 149–153
    turnover rate, 2
    See also departing executive directors;
        interim executive directors; long-
        tenured executive directors; new
        executive directors
Executive Transition Management model
    (ETM), 9–10, 12–14
exit packages, 43, 126–127

finalists
    background checks, 90, 92
    and departing executive director, 94
    interview sample agenda for, 95t
    job offer, 98, 99t
    references, 87, 90, 91t
    rejection notification, 100
    selecting, 87, 88t–89t, 93–96, 97t

Following the Leader (Redington and
  Vickers), 124
funders
  communicating with, 43–44, 45*t*,
    142–143
  developing new, 14–15, 17
  and search, 75
  strategic directions/plans survey of,
    51–52, 52*t*
  support during transition, 4

Gilmore, Tom, 2
Guidestar, 43

high-performing agencies, shifts in goals and
  strategies of, 16–17

incumbent executive directors. *See* departing
  executive directors
interim executive directors
  advantages of, 11–12, 130, 131
  for agencies in decline, 18–19, 130
  board member as, 129–130
  sources of candidates, 130
internal candidates, 125–126
interviews, courtesy, 126
interviews, first-round
  behavioral interviewing, 84, 85*t*
  conducting, 86
  documenting impressions after, 86
  location of, 82–83
  questions, 82*t*–83*t*, 83–84
  and references, 81
  role assignments for, 84
  scheduling, 82
  selling position during, 66
interviews, second-round
  background checks, 90, 92
  board of directors screening, 94–96
  departing executive director involvement,
    94
  reference checks, 90, 91*t*
  sample agenda for, 95*t*
  selecting finalists for, 87, 88*t*–89*t*,
    93–96, 97*t*
  staff involvement, 93–94

job announcements
  and diversity of candidate pool, 75–76
  drafting, 66
  information contained in, 70–71
  posting, 71, 73
  sample, 67*t*–69*t*, 71
  as selling tool, 63, 65–66
Jones, Karen Gaskins, 2

leadership agenda
  and board of directors, 56–57
  and candidate profile, 58
  importance of, 57
  sample, 56*t*–57*t*
  steps to arrive at, 54, 55*t*, 56
  and Thrive committee, 107–108
  updating agency's, 44, 45–47, 47*t*, 49–54,
    50*t*–51*t*, 52*t*
  and vision, 46, 53, 54
long-tenured executive directors
  challenge of replacing, 19–20, 119–120
  coaching for, 28
  and departure-defined succession
    planning, 120–122
  exit packages for, 43, 126–127
  and interim executive directors, 131
  personal story of replacement of, 135–137
  and strategic leadership development,
    122–123
  time frame for, 119

Main Street Services, 20–21
*Managing Transitions: Making the Most of
  Change,* 10
mission. *See* vision statements
morale. *See under* staff
multiculturalism. *See* diversity

NeighborWorks America, 1, 23
networking
  importance of, 66
  as professional development component,
    117
  role of, 72*t*, 73, 74*t*, 75
neutral zone (Bridges), 10, 11
New Beginnings, 18–19
new executive directors
  assessment of, 25, 108–109, 110*t*–113*t*,
    118
  and board of directors, 10, 29, 104,
    114–115, 146

groomed by departing executive director, 127–128
hiring announcement sample letter, 105*t*
and leadership agenda, 107–108
offer letter template, 99*t*
orientation of, 104, 106*t,* 107, 146
performance goals, 107–108, 108*t,* 118
professional development for, 116–117, 146
resignations, 141, 145
and staff, 64*t*
start date of, 61
terms of employment, 43, 87, 98
nonprofit agencies
addressing funding issues, 14–15, 17
addressing organizational issues, 25
assessment of needs, 42
culture of, 146
in decline, 18–19, 25, 130
high-performing, 16–17
importance of, 3
updating leadership agenda, 44, 45–47, 47*t,* 49–54, 50*t*–51*t,* 52*t*

Pivot phase
overview of, 10, 25–26, 135
step-by-step, 61–101
See also specific subjects such as candidates and finalists
Prepare phase
overview of, 10, 24–25, 135
step-by-step, 31–60
See also transition and search committees
professional development
importance of, 25, 65
and new executive director, 116–117, 146
and strategic leader development, 122–123

recruiters. *See* consultants
recruitment. *See* search
Redington, Emily, 124, 143
references
of candidates, 29, 82, 86
of finalists, 87, 90, 91*t*
questions arising from, 81
resumes
acknowledging, 77, 79*t*
sorting, 77, 78*t,* 79–80

salary. *See* compensation
search
departing executive director's role, 35–36, 94, 144
difficulties faced, 1, 3–4
and diversity of candidate pool, 75–76
geographic area covered, 71, 73
job announcement, 63, 65–66, 67*t*–69*t*
and networking, 66, 73, 74*t,* 75
personal story of, 135–137
preparation, 11–12
sample plan, 72*t*
screening sequence, 77, 78*t,* 79–81
staff's role, 10, 28–29
time frame for, 61
See also candidates; job announcements
search tool samples
agenda for finalists' interviews and decision-making meeting, 95*t*
behavioral interviewing, 85*t*
candidate rating form, 88*t*–89*t*
first-round interview questions, 82*t*–83*t*
job announcement, 67*t*–69*t*
letter of acknowledgment to candidates, 79*t*
networking memo to board of directors and staff, 74*t*
offer letter, 99*t*
recruitment plan, 72*t*
reference checking, 91*t*
rejection letter, 100t
screening sequence, 78*t*
selecting candidate, 97*t*
skill development. *See* professional development
staff
as candidate, 35, 125–126
communicating with, 28, 43–44, 45*t,* 141–142
early input from, 10
and emergency leadership plan, 123
and finalists, 93–94
morale, 4, 26, 62–63, 64*t*
and new executive director, 64*t,* 104
personal story of involvement by, 137
recruitment efforts of, 75
sample networking memo to, 74*t*
and screening process, 81

strategic directions/plans survey of, 49–50, 50*t*–51*t*
and transition committee, 12–13, 28–29, 34–35
stakeholders
communicating with, 43–44, 45*t*
and finalists' interviews, 92–97
See also specific groups
start-up agencies, 15
strategic directions/plans
and assessment of executive director, 109
and embracing diversity, 128–129
importance of, 44, 46
relationship to candidate profile, 54
setting, 28
and strategic leader development, 122–123
strategic directions/plans surveys
of board of directors, 46–47, 47*t*
of departing executive directors, 49
of funders, 51–52, 52*t*
of staff, 49–50, 50*t*–51*t*
strategic leader development, 122–123
succession planning, 6–7, 120–123, 149–153
sustainability audits, 121

Third Sector New England, 1
Thrive committee
dissolution of, 117–118
membership, 103
and new executive director's orientation, 104
and new executive director's performance, 107–108
and new executive director's professional development, 116–117
Thrive phase
overview of, 10, 25, 135
step-by-step, 103–118
transition
elements, 12, 27–30
opportunities offered by, 139, 140

phases, 5, 10–11, 12
See also Pivot phase; Prepare phase; Thrive phase
time frame for, 61, 119, 121
types of, 4–5, 14–15

transition and search committees
and board of directors, 27
budget for, 42
decision-making process, 38–39
duties, 24, 32–33, 39, 81
duties of chair, 33–34
first meeting, 36, 38, 42–44
first meeting sample agenda, 37*t*
forming, 31–32
leadership agenda and performance goals, 107
membership, 33–35, 38
personal story of, 135–137
rules, 38
team building, 38
and Thrive committee, 103
workplan and schedule, 39, 40*t*–41*t*
TransitionGuides, 1, 23
transparency, 28, 43–44, 45*t*
Treasure Island Memorial Foundation, 14–15
turnaround transitions
description of need for, 18–19
and interim executive directors, 130
and time frame, 25

unplanned departures, 6–7, 123, 149–153

Vickers, Donn, 124, 143
vision statements
and leadership agenda, 46, 53, 54
as selling point of position, 63
updating, 32, 33, 35
volunteers as information sources, 53

web recruitment, 71, 73

More Results-Oriented Resources
from Fieldstone Alliance

Practical books are just one of the resources Fieldstone Alliance has to offer. We also provide consulting, training, and demonstration projects that help nonprofits, funders, networks, and communities achieve greater impact.

As a nonprofit ourselves, we know the challenges that you face. In all our services, we draw on our extensive experience to provide solutions that work:

EXPERT CONSULTATION

Our staff and network of affiliated consultants are recognized nonprofit leaders, authors, and experts with deep experience in managing organizations, teaching, training, conducting research, and leading community initiatives. We provide assessment, planning, financial strategy, collaboration, and capacity-building services. Contracts range from short-term assessments to the management of multi-year initiatives.

PROVEN TRAINING

Training can be a powerful change strategy when well designed. Our experienced staff, authors, and network of experts from across the United States provide practical, customized training for nonprofits, foundations, and consultants. From one-hour keynote addresses to multi-session programs, we offer expertise in various aspects of capacity building, nonprofit management, leadership, collaboration, and community development. Coupling training with books and follow-up support increases retention and application of what is learned.

DEMONSTRATION PROJECTS

Fieldstone Alliance conducts research and hosts demonstration projects that have promise for improving performance and results in the nonprofit sector. Through this work we mine best practices, package the findings into practical, easy-to-apply tools, and disseminate them throughout the sector.

To find out more, call 1-800-274-6024. Or visit www.FieldstoneAlliance.org.

▸ **SEE MORE BOOKS AND FREE RESOURCES**

Free Resources

GET FREE MANAGEMENT TIPS!

Sign-up for *Nonprofit Tools You Can Use,* Fieldstone Alliance's free e-newsletter. In each issue (arriving twice a month), we feature a free management tool or idea to help you and your nonprofit be more effective.

Content comes from our award-winning books, our consultant's direct experience, and from other experts in the field. Each issue focuses on a specific topic and includes practical actions for putting the information to use.

There are more than 70 great issues in the archive!

ONLINE RESOURCES

Here are other free resources you'll find on our web site:

Articles
In-depth information on key nonprofit management issues.

Assessment Tools
See how your organization or collaboration is doing relative to characteristics of a successful nonprofit.

Research Reports
See research that was done to inform our demonstration projects and consulting practice.

Related Books

Seven Turning Points
Leading Through Pivotal Transitions in Organizational Life

To remain strong and effective, organizations must periodically adjust their leadership, management, structure, governance, and operating style to fit their changed circumstances. *Seven Turning Points* identifies key times when nonprofits must reassess the way they operate and make fundamental changes or risk decline.

by Susan Gross | 120 pp | 2009 | ISBN 978-0-940069-73-2 | order no. 069732

The Nonprofit Strategy Revolution
Real-Time Strategic Planning in a Rapid-Response World

This ground-breaking guide offers a compelling alternative to traditional strategic planning. You'll find new ideas for how to form strategies, and the tools and framework needed to infuse strategic thinking throughout your organization. The result: your nonprofit will be more strategic in thought and action on a daily basis. When the next opportunity (or challenge) comes along, you'll be able to respond swiftly and thoughtfully.

by David La Piana | 208 pp | 2008 | ISBN 978-0-940069-65-7 | order no. 069657

Generations
The Challenge of a Lifetime for Your Nonprofit

What happens when a management team of all Baby Boomers leaves within a five year stretch? Peter Brinckerhoff tells you what generational changes to expect and how to plan for them. You'll find in-depth information for each area of your organization—staff, board, volunteers, clients, marketing, technology, and finances.

by Peter Brinckerhoff | 232 pp | 2007 | ISBN 978-0-940069-55-8 | order no. 069555

Financial Leadership for Nonprofit Executives
Guiding Your Organization to Long-term Success

Provides executives with a practical guide to protecting and growing the assets of their organizations while accomplishing as much mission as possible with those resources.

by Jeanne Bell & Elizabeth Schaffer | 144 pp | 2005 | ISBN 978-0-940069-44-2 | order no. 06944X

Benchmarking for Nonprofits
How to Measure, Manage, and Improve Results

This book defines a formal, systematic, and reliable way to benchmark (the ongoing process of measuring your organization against leaders), from preparing your organization to measuring performance and implementing best practices.

by Jason Saul | 144 pp | 2004 | ISBN 978-0-940069-43-5 | order no. 069431

The Five Life Stages of Nonprofit Organizations
Where You Are, Where You're Going, & What to Expect When You Get There

Shows you what's "normal" for each development stage which helps you plan for transitions, stay on track, and avoid unnecessary struggles. Includes an assessment.

by Judith Sharken Simon with J. Terence Donovan
128 pp | 2001 | ISBN 978-0-940069-22-0 | order no. 069229

The Manager's Guide to Program Evaluation
Planning, Contracting, and Managing for Useful Results

Explains how to plan and manage an evaluation that will help identify your organization's successes, share information with key audiences, and improve services.

by Paul W. Mattessich, PhD | 112 pp | 2003 | ISBN 978-0-940069-38-1 | order no. 069385

Nonprofit Stewardship
A Better Way to Lead Your Mission-Based Organization

You may lead a nonprofit, but it's not your organization; it belongs to the community it serves. You are the steward—the manager of resources that belong to someone else. The stewardship model of leadership can help you make decisions that are best for the people you serve by keeping your mission foremost.

by Peter C. Brinckerhoff | 272 pp | 2004 | ISBN 978-0-940069-42-8 | order no. 069423

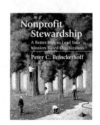

Strategic Planning Workbook, Revised and Updated

Chart a wise course for your nonprofit's future. This time-tested workbook gives you practical step-by-step guidance, real-life examples, and one nonprofit's complete strategic plan.

by Bryan W. Barry | 144 pp | 1997 | ISBN 978-0-940069-07-7 | order no. 069075